T0128475

Ariella's Miracle

*The Lioness of the Lord—How Prayer and the
Prophetic Delivered a Baby Girl from Death*

Patrick J. Lenney

WESTBOW
PRESS®
A DIVISION OF THOMAS NELSON
& ZONDERVAN

WestBow Press books may be ordered through booksellers or by contacting:

WestBow Press
A Division of Thomas Nelson & Zondervan
1663 Liberty Drive
Bloomington, IN 47403
www.westbowpress.com
1 (866) 928-1240

ISBN: 978-1-9736-4638-9 (sc)
ISBN: 978-1-9736-4639-6 (hc)
ISBN: 978-1-9736-4637-2 (e)

Library of Congress Control Number: 2018913811

Print information available on the last page.

WestBow Press rev. date: 12/07/2018

Dedication

Ariella, our baby girl, Daddy and Mommy love you. From the day of your arrival, you have given us more joy than any father and mother have a right to. We have never witnessed anyone with your tenacity, spirit, energy, and personality; you are fearfully and wonderfully made by God—unique in every way. One day, you will be old enough to read this, and I cannot imagine the questions you will have for me and Mommy. We look forward to sharing with you all God has done in your life so far and to explore all He has in store for you.

With this book, Daddy and Mommy wanted to praise God for saving your life and returning you to us. You have a story that needs telling, and you will undoubtedly tell others and inspire them to trust God with all their hearts.

Again, Daddy and Mommy love you, and we will always be here for you. We cannot adequately put words together to describe our love and affection for you; it is impossible to describe. We can only say that it is the closest we have ever gotten to understanding in a small measure what God the

Father must have felt when Jesus died on the cross for us. We are amazed at your lioness-like fighting spirit that inspires all who meet you. Daddy and Mommy speak life and power to you and over you, and we are comforted that God has you in His loving arms. God intimately knows you. He has good plans for you and thoughts of peace to give you an incredible future and hope.

Most important, our heavenly Father, our Lord and Savior Jesus Christ loves you, and He is with you always. He was with you on August 19, 2016, and held you safely, and He walks with you every day. You hold a special place in God's heart, and you are so valuable to Him.

Baby girl, Daddy and Mommy love you!

Contents

Introduction

My hope and prayer in writing Ariella's story is to inspire people to believe in God and in Him for the miraculous. Before I gave my life to Christ, I believed in me. As a Marine, I believed in my military leaders, my government, and certain systems. In hindsight, I believed somewhat blindly, confidently placing my belief in them. That would change for me when I placed my belief in God.

In October 1994, I visited a small black church outside the Marine Corps base in Quantico, Virginia. When the preacher spoke, it was as though I were the only person in the church; he was speaking directly to me. The Word of God touched my heart, and I experienced His love that day.

At the end of the sermon, the preacher invited those of us who had not accepted Jesus Christ into our hearts. He said, "Jesus died for you. He is able to forgive you, and He will make you into a new creature. Come to the altar and give your life to Him today."

When I heard his words, I told myself, *Stay in your seat. Don't get up!* It was as close to an out-of-body experience as I have ever had. I was telling myself not to go, but my legs stood, and I was walking toward the front of the church. Awaiting me was a young minister who asked me, "What do you want the Lord to do for you?" With tears streaming down my face, I told him, "I want Jesus to forgive me." In that moment, I richly felt the love and presence of God, and to have that sense of peace and purpose was a miracle. I did not just know of Him; I also believed in Him.

Believing is a powerful force. Belief causes people to achieve amazing feats, overcome the most difficult challenges, and experience unexplained success. Belief is the pathway to the miraculous for those who believe in God. Ariella's story serves as a pathway, a powerful message of faith, hope, and grace glorifying God while drawing people to Him and believe in Him for miracles. *To believe*—those two words sum it up.

Over the years, I have pastored overseas and in the United States. Though not perfectly, I have lived a life of faith and have always found my anchor in Christ. I have always had a pastor's heart and a heart for men; I remain involved in men's ministry today. I am privileged to know men and women of faith—fathers and mothers in the gospel who have invested their lives in mine, and I have witnessed God's ability to change people's hearts. Seeing people transformed by God's love never gets old, and witnessing people moved to believe is a gift.

I hope through this book that your heart and mind will be transformed and that you will adopt an attitude of expectation for the miraculous in your life. God is still doing miracles; we hear about them all the time. We are even amazed and overjoyed when we see it in others' testimonies, so why do we stop short?

I sense the challenge is that we believe God can do miracles but that we are not convinced He will do them for us. Why have people stopped believing? Is it the pressures of life, a wounded or hurting heart, perhaps anger, or frustration, or fear—fear of asking God for the miraculous? Believing is a stretching of our faith, and it is often left unpursued. I have heard the testimonies of those who have experienced miracles and know well the encouragement and empowerment they provide. They encouraged me when I needed it most. There comes with it a realization of hope that it can happen for you. In telling Ariella's story, I feel moved to inspire you to desperately seek God not only in the most difficult of circumstances but also in every day of your life for the miraculous.

The Holy Spirit placed this passion in my heart to share Ariella's story in this way. Believe me when I say I tried to ignore it. Writing a book is an incredible undertaking, and I used about every excuse I could to avoid it. When would I have the time to write a book? I asked, *Lord, how can I tell this story?* I just kept coming back to the notion that I had to commit to getting it down on paper. I started taking notes, gathering numerous testimonies and accounts of the people involved, and collecting all the medical notes related to Ariella. What began as an outline turned into this incredible journey into the power of believing, a type of believing we all are capable of each day. This believing becomes our default fighting position planted in God, who can do anything we need.

Nora, my wife, and I took this fighting position for Ariella. We arrived at it differently, but we arrived at it in agreement and believing and desperately seeking God to perform the miraculous. Our family, friends, and the community of faith joined us in this fighting position, and it became a strategic, prophetic voice and force against evil. This innumerable fighting force bombarded the kingdom of heaven, and God placed His works on display through Ariella.

This default fighting position of believing helped me write Ariella's story. I have felt the presence of God helping me and bringing to my mind the integral parts of my daughter's story. I was continually reminded and encouraged by the gospel of Jesus Christ and His love for all humanity. I was mindful of

God's love for my family, and I was inspired by the testimonies of those who witnessed it. Throughout, I gained strength from the opportunity to proclaim God's love by sharing Ariella's experience. The same enduring love that raised Christ from the dead raised my beautiful Ariella.

When Ariella's story went public, local media coverage shared her story, and it reached the western New York region. However, because of the nature of short news stories, it could not tell the entire story. Her story began to spread beyond the local news and made its way to a larger audience. It was televised on the Christian Broadcasting Network on June 11, 2018, on a program entitled "Parents Hold to Promise for Miracle." It reached millions of homes and viewers throughout the world.

Nora and I share Ariella's story with others including churches that ask us to visit. We are grateful to experience the hope it provides to those who hear it. We are blessed to hear the testimonies of people who have experienced God's mercy and miracles of their own. And regrettably, we hear the painful stories of those who have lost children or family members through all manner of circumstances. These are the most difficult and challenging realities. Believing and remaining in our fighting position becomes much tougher, but God's grace heals us and keeps us in position. Nora and I are humbled to be a part of people's lives in this way.

These difficult circumstances are another reason I was led to write Ariella's story. The hurting hearts of those who have retreated into despair need restoration. Believing in God and the miraculous strengthens us to endure and keep fighting. Proclaiming the Word of God, prayer, and prophesying to dry and dead places is our armor.

For those of you who have lost children, take the only consolation I could receive in my darkest hour—your precious children are in the loving arms of Jesus. They are walking in the heavenly places not experiencing pain or hurt; they do not feel let down by you, and they do not feel sickness or sadness. They are loved, at peace, and with our Savior. I realize these words are of little consolation to parents who lost their loved ones, but there was a time in Ariella's experience that Jesus's promises were the only words of consolation I could receive.

So many of us are seeking God's miraculous touch in the face of adversity. We struggle to understand why these difficulties occur. In an effort to speak to those who are hurting, I am convinced there is no rhyme, reason, or quick antidote for tragedy. It can be attributed to bad decisions, youth, lack of experience, a terrible accident, or evil. It can be unexpected sickness or illness. No matter the kind of tragedy, these events can become faith-filled walks though they can have horrific or joyous and often unexplainable outcomes. I sense today more than ever in my life how incredibly precious, complicated, and distinct our lives are. Life happens to us all, and I learned that tragedy can happen quickly. This is where tragedy and belief collide.

As you read this book, I ask you to place yourselves in it. Find a character you identify with and ask God to reveal His heart to you. Obviously, in this book, my wife and I are the parents who adore their child with all their heart. You may be the parent, grandparent, family member, friend, or physician. And suddenly this kind of tragic event occurs. The impact on a family can be devastating. For those of you who have experienced this or worse, you know this too well.

After the shock and trauma of dealing with the initial blows, all that was left for our family was our belief in the miraculous. We all have faith in something whether in God, ourselves, professionals, power, organizations, or systems. For us, it was faith through the power of prayer for a miracle. It was faith grounded through the Word and promises of God and prophetically spoken into existence by us and the community of faith.

All of you who need a miracle should bang the doors of heaven down, block out the world, and ask God to do the amazing. Be specific, be big, and believe.

This book is based on the true story of one little girl's miracle, Ariella's miracle. God raised her from the dead and caused her to inspire a world. I intend on telling it to all those who will listen. I believe that one day through her story, Ariella will proclaim the Word of the Lord to God's people. God still answers prayers, and He still performs miracles. May Ariella's story encourage and inspire you with renewed faith and hope in God to believe in Him for the miraculous—to believe.

Chapter

1

The First Day (August 19– 20)—An Ordinary Day

For I know the thoughts that I think toward you, saith the LORD, *thoughts of peace, and not of evil, to give you an expected end.*
—Jeremiah 29:11 KJV

I woke up the morning of August 19, 2016 at about 7:30 a.m. feeling troubled and even fearful. I had had a dream I knew was spiritual, and it concerned me so much that I had to check on my daughter, Ariella. When I went to her room, she was lying there sleeping very peacefully so much so that I placed my hand on her chest to make sure she was breathing. When I returned to bed, I joined my wife, Nora, and wondered if I should share my dream with her.

God speaks to me primarily through His Word, but He often gives me dreams I know provide me spiritual insight, direction, and warnings, and He always seems to do it right before I wake up. I attribute this to His wanting me to remember the details of the dream.

On that morning, I lay there going over the details of this dream so I would not forget them. Of course, I can work through many of my dreams quickly and chalk them up to some bad food the night before. But many of my dreams are spiritual and serve as another way God speaks to me. Dreams are ordinarily described as good or bad, but I consider them spiritual or not. My spiritual dreams stand out, and I sense their significance immediately; I consider their meaning in the light of God's Word, and they most always move me to pray about my actions and response to them. The dream I had that morning was different. It possessed an urgency unlike any dream I had had before.

In the dream, standing before me was an evil presence, gray and blurry, with red eyes. Darkness surrounded us. I knew this demonic presence was feminine, and that was confirmed when she spoke: "I am going to take your daughter."

I replied, "No you are not!" I made that declaration with authority and reached out as if to snatch from her any power she had in those words. The dream was that quick, and it was as real as though I was awake and in person. Lying there with my wife, I decided the dream was so concerning that I had to share it with her.

"Honey, I had a terrible dream I have to tell you about so we'll know how to pray."

She replied, "I knew something was going on when you got up and went over to check on Ariella."

She listened intently to my dream, and she agreed it was something God was sharing with me. Nora has giftings in the prophetic and a sensitivity to the voice of the Lord. We talked about what the dream meant, and we agreed to be prayerful and watchful over our children.

We got out of bed and began to take on the day. We had breakfast with the kids and went back upstairs to clean the kids' rooms and fold clothes. We had a lot going on; it was a significant time of transition for us. I had just landed a position as a responder on the Veterans' and Military Crisis Line, Veteran Affairs, in Canandaigua, New York. I was a counselor for veterans who were suicidal or in crisis. We were getting our home ready to sell in the midst of buying a new home thirty miles south and much closer to my new job. I had a contractor coming to the house around 9:00 that morning, and I was going to a leadership conference at Lakeshore Church at 11:00. I was also wrapping up a master's in divinity degree at Northeastern Seminary, and attending this leadership conference was an accredited course. I was getting semester hour credits while hearing powerful biblical teaching—a win-win.

I had been involved in ministry since 1997, and I always wanted a master's in divinity and to have the rich experience of doing expository study of the scriptures in an academic setting. I always strived to do expository preaching and teaching, and I felt being at seminary and learning under theologians and scholars would further prepare me for my next ministry steps. It was a very busy time in our lives, and it was a full day.

Nora and I were still upstairs picking up our bedroom; our two little girls, Gianna and Ariella, were playing in their room adjacent to ours. Gianna was five, and Ariella was sixteen months old. My nineteen-year-old son, Jacob, and twelve-year-old son, Ethan, were still asleep. I looked out of the window and saw that Paul, my contractor, had pulled in the driveway and was making his way to the backyard.

"Nora, I'm going out to meet Paul."

"Okay, see you in a little bit."

I walked downstairs, went onto the back deck, and went down two additional sets of stairs past our aboveground pool. Paul and I began talking about the work he and his crew were going to do that day. He wanted to show me what he had in mind to beautify the front of the home. We walked around to the front, and he shared with me how he was going to paint and mulch, and we agreed on a plan. He and I had done business in the past, and I enjoyed talking with him.

It was a beautiful, warm, and sunny day. Paul and I sat in the two large lawn chairs in the front yard. We enjoyed talking for a moment about my selling the home, ways to declutter it, and our moving plans. We were planning to move to our new home in a few months. Paul agreed to take that effort on also and move us. Paul was and remains an incredible blessing to our family.

As we sat there soaking in the day for a few minutes, I heard a scream like I had never heard before. I knew something was very wrong. It was terror filled. Nora was screaming, "Patrick! Patrick!"

I was startled. Paul and I jumped to our feet. I ran as fast as I could into the front door and saw my wife holding my baby Ariella; she was blue and not conscious. I was in shock. Everything stopped. My heart sank, and we frantically ran to the living room and laid her on the floor. Nora began to do CPR as I arched Ariella's neck.

Ethan heard the commotion and ran into the living room. I yelled, "Ethan, call 911!"

He dialed it quickly and handed me the phone. At first, I was trying to help my wife and talk with the 911 dispatcher with the phone to my ear. That did not work, so I put the phone on speaker and laid it on the floor next to us. While we were getting instructions on how to properly perform CPR on our baby, my wife was praying in the Spirit and asking God to help Ariella. Amazingly, she did that the entire time she was doing the compressions and breathing.

I was pleading, "God, help my baby girl! My baby is dying, Lord."

The 911 dispatcher remained calm; he instructed us slowly and deliberately. He said, "Help is on the way."

Ariella had made her way downstairs and had apparently followed me out the back door, walked down the steps, and went into the pool when Paul and I were in the front yard. Nora's mother sensors went off because it seemed a little too quiet. She thought Ariella had gone downstairs to play with her toys as she so often did.

Nora had called out, "Ariella! What are you doing? Where are you?"

Nora sent Gianna to locate her. Gianna saw the back door open; she went outside and saw Ariella in the pool. Gianna ran and told Nora, "Ariella's in the pool, Mommy."

Nora bolted outside, and to her horror, she saw Ariella floating face down. She ran around the pool and grabbed Ariella out. She went inside screaming my name.

Terror overcame me. I asked Jacob to take Ethan and Gianna upstairs to keep them from experiencing this horrific moment any further. There is no deeper sense of powerlessness for parents than to see their children hurt, and it's magnified when they could die. It is not supposed to happen like that.

As Nora was doing CPR, Ariella spit up some curdled milk from the bottle she had had that morning, and her skin seemed to be moving from pale blue to fleshy pink. When the paramedics arrived, they instructed Nora to continue with the compressions as they unpacked their medical equipment. We stood and stepped back relieved to see a little color coming back to Ariella. That relief was removed as the paramedic exclaimed, "I have no pulse," and asked us to move completely out of the way.

The paramedic team worked on her for what seemed to be an hour though I am sure it was only a few minutes. They gave her medications and continued to work on her without letting up. They shocked her three times. I was in a fog. They placed an object in her leg and kept working on her. They decided to get Ariella to Strong Memorial Hospital in Rochester, New York. We were at least twenty minutes away. It was unclear if they had a pulse when we departed the house, and they had no encouraging words.

As we came outside our home, several television crews, neighbors, friends, volunteer firefighters, and responders were filling the front yard and street. Nora and I ran alongside Ariella. The paramedics asked if I wanted to ride in the ambulance with her to the hospital.

"Yes!" I exclaimed.

They loaded her in. Jacob had the children.

Nora said, "I'll follow in the car."

I jumped in the passenger seat of the ambulance, and off we went. As we traveled down the road, the driver talked to me; she was trying to keep me calm and be supportive. She told me she would tell me anything important; I hung on every word of the first responders in the back of the ambulance listening for any words of hope.

Every couple of minutes, I would shout back to them, "Do you have a pulse? Is she breathing?"

They told me what they were doing with Ariella, all the steps they were taking to help her. Having been a counselor for over two years on the Veterans' Suicide Hotline, I knew the importance and value of having that kind of calm presence; their calm and professionalism was incredible in these intense and emotionally charged moments. I learned later that it had taken the paramedics five minutes to arrive. Nora was doing the compressions for the entire time, and it then took four more minutes for the paramedics to get a rhythm after shocking Ariella three times. When we arrived at the hospital, it was reported that Ariella was wheezing. I wondered, *Does that mean she's breathing, or is it an involuntary bodily function?*

When we arrived at Strong Memorial's ER, there was an organized frenzy as they whisked Ariella to the nearest triage room. Nora and I sat right outside Ariella's space separated by a curtain several feet away. Physicians and nurses were moving quickly, communicating rapidly and in an orderly fashion, and running through Ariella's vitals as they tried to help her.

After several minutes, the lead ER physician came out to talk with us. I nervously asked, "How is she?"

"Based on my initial assessment and CT scan, Ariella had suffered significant loss of brain function and was experiencing seizures due to oxygen loss to her brain."

He shared this devastating news matter of factly; Nora and I felt numb. We consoled each other. I thought this could not be the plan God had for Ariella. Jeremiah 29:11 (NIV) declares, "God knows the plans he has for us, they are of peace, they are good; not evil." *How can this be God's plan for Ariella? Surely this cannot be part of that plan!*

The lead ER physician was very concerned; he must have had to deliver that kind of report many times, and it cannot be easy to see that kind of tragedy each day. He was courteous, clear, and concise; he was focused on getting back to caring for Ariella.

A sheriff stood with us in the triage area. I first thought he was part of hospital security, but a few minutes later, he talked with me about what had happened. It was apparent that he was not there only to get a report but also to observe my wife and me. An ER social worker also gathered information and was certainly observing our presentation. The sheriff and social worker were kind and certainly doing their duty. Nora recalls our discussions, but I do not remember either conversation well, and I am not sure what that must have looked like to them. What we learned next from the sheriff stopped my wife and me in our tracks.

Chapter

2

Underwater for Ten Minutes

*When thou passest through the waters, I will be with
thee; and through the rivers, they shall not overflow
thee: when thou walkest through the fire, thou shalt not
be burned; neither shall the flame kindle upon thee.*
—Isaiah 43:2 KJV

We learned later in the day from the sheriff's office that Ariella had been underwater for ten minutes. The sheriff told us, "Your neighbor has a security camera with tape." Hearing his words unsettled me and made me cringe. My baby girl had been underwater from 9:23 to 9:33. I am still horrified at what Ariella must have experienced—the fear and fighting for her life. Was she yelling for Mommy or Daddy? I just kept responding to my own thoughts with

God, help us, please! Nora and I were focused on Ariella; we were listening intently to the doctor, but I was still in shock and disbelief that this had actually happened. *God, how could this have happened? How did it happen so quickly? We were right there! Had I left the back door open? God, please help my little girl!*

How does God do it? In Isaiah 43:2, God told the three Hebrew boys that though they would be engulfed by flames and intense heat for a prolonged time, they would not be overcome. In the natural world, that just does not make sense; many had perished in the flames by the king's directive, but God's spoken word set the three Hebrew boys apart and saved them from certain death. Ariella needed that kind of protection; that was when Nora got into her default fighting position of belief.

I was still clamoring, *God, Ariella was underwater for ten minutes. I know you are able to, so will you protect my daughter from the water as you did the Hebrew boys from the fire?* I was walking up the hill to get into the fighting position. I had not arrived yet. Everything in me was struggling with those ten minutes. I know what happens when someone is underwater that long without oxygen. She could not swim as she would have needed to. She would not be able to get oxygen to her brain. She would not be able to stop her lungs from being filled with pool water. She could not stop the seizures. My baby girl needed God to do the miraculous.

I cried aloud, "Oh God, God, God, God!" I screamed internally, *Father, Father, help her! Lord, can you protect her brain and lungs from being overcome? Help my daughter, Lord.*

The lead ER physician told us that Ariella had been sedated and intubated; an electroencephalogram (EEG) was on her head to measure brain activity, and they were going to continue to work on her and perform tests. He expressed concern about what he described as Ariella's brain being swollen and then described what often happened in injuries like hers: "The brain continues to swell; it has nowhere to go, and then it moves down the neck, cuts off oxygen, and results in death."

The lead ER physician reported in the medical records that Ariella had suffered cerebral edema, seizures, cardiac arrest, acute respiratory failure, and anoxic brain damage. He said Ariella was unresponsive. He said, "There's a high probability of imminent or life-threatening deterioration due to cardiac failure, circulatory failure, respiratory failure, and trauma." Nora and I sunk into chairs they provided to us feeling powerless to help our baby girl.

An hour later, 10:41 a.m., Ariella continued to have seizures that the medical team was working to reduce or eliminate. At 12:41 p.m., three hours of sheer terror had passed. My wife and I were looking at everything with thousand-yard stares. Ariella was intubated to avoid respiratory failure and to protect her airway. A CT scan showed loss of gray-white matter differentiation at her basal ganglia. This part of the brain is associated with a variety of functions including control of voluntary motor movements, procedural learning, routine behaviors, eye movement, cognition, and emotion. After hearing all these voices, it was hard for me to stay in the default fighting position of believing. Thank God for wives who love God. Nora and I agreed that believing was the only place we could fight from.

At 1:30 p.m., Ariella was moved from the ER to PICU (pediatric intensive care unit) and placed in her own room. The first person we met was nurse Jen Ireland, who cared for Ariella so gently. She briefed us on what was going on with Ariella and asked us to step outside. She said she would come for us and bring us in when they had her settled. Little did we know at the time, but Jen was a believer in Christ and a member of our church. It is amazing how God provides those types of grace connections in difficult times.

Nora and I agreed to step outside for a moment, get some air, and come right back in. We sat on a bench in front of the hospital. I needed to contact the men of God in my life and solicit their prayers for Ariella. I had to call my father in the gospel. I called Pastor John Marshall, my pastor since 1997, and shared with him the news about Ariella. I did not get it out to him without breaking down. It still amazes me how he responded. He and his wife, Loretta, were together, and we put our phones on speaker. Pastor Marshall was oddly calm, and as always was his way, he asked if he could pray with Nora and me. We welcomed that, and he started to pray. He prayed the promises of God, spoke His Word, and asked Him to bless and heal Ariella.

Pastor Marshall said, "You remain in faith and call me with updates. I'll get everyone notified, and the churches will be praying for you."

He leads an apostolic ministry that has churches throughout the United States and overseas. I knew what he meant, and we greatly appreciated it. I have been under good leadership in my twenty-three years in the Marine Corps as well as in ministry. I know no man of God with greater faith. Pastor Marshall reminded us to remain in the fighting position of believing.

I told him, "I will sir. Thank you."

Nora asked, "Did you sense how calm he was? As if he knew or felt she was going to be okay?"

"Yes I did. His calm and assurance went straight to my heart, and my faith has been lifted. He spoke to us to believe!"

If only for a moment, I felt some relief from the heaviness I had been feeling all morning. Nora and I embraced and made our way back to the PICU.

In the PICU, an amazing team of physicians, nurses, and staff took charge of Ariella's care. They kept her sedated and on a cooling blanket. They monitored the swelling of her brain by ensuring a good attachment of the EEG to her head. They had to shave parts of her scalp to accomplish that, and they catheterized her. Nora and I hovered in Ariella's room and listened to every word. We prayed, waited, paced, and asked God to help our little girl recover.

That afternoon, the lead PICU physician asked to speak with Nora and me. She led us and a resident to a holding area; we sat, and she gave us the worst prognosis.

"Ariella suffered significant brain damage, and the little girl you knew, you will not know again. A certain area of her brain is so damaged that if she survives, she will never again feel, or think, or have emotions like a normal child. She is most likely neurologically devastated and is also at risk of organ failure."

The baby girl we knew was energetic and independent, and she loved to sing and dance. Her laughter was contagious, and she loved to be the center of attention on every cell phone video. I asked, "What did you say? This doesn't sound possible. How do you know that?"

Nora and I sat in shock and disbelief at the doctor's words. We must have looked like boxers who had left their guards down and had just kept taking face shots.

She said, "Ariella will not have motor skills. She will not be able to walk, talk, or feed herself."

Hers was an experienced voice; she was the lead physician in the PICU and the resident expert on Ariella's care. She must have seen such cases many times before.

I thought, *God, this cannot be true. Don't let this be true.*

She told us, "The next seventy-two hours are most crucial. If we don't see the swelling in the brain lessen, she may not make it through the night."

We were visibly shaken trying to absorb every medical fact we had just heard. We had blank stares looking around the room and at each other. We were crying and had aching in our hearts words cannot describe.

But it was then that Nora assumed her fighting position. She looked at me and then at the doctor. "No, that is not God's plan for Ariella. I'm sorry, but I cannot accept that. No!"

I remembered the dream I had had that morning; the evil spirit threatened to take my daughter, but I defiantly responded, "No you are not!" and snatched her back with confidence. I saw the evil presence flee. I said no. Nora said no. We agreed before and after concerning Ariella's future on a spiritual level that the human mind cannot perform—God was helping us.

From that moment, Nora walked in unwavering faith that God would heal our Ariella, but I was a work in progress. I was making my way to the fighting position. I will talk more about that later. It was not that I did not believe God could heal her; I just could not dismiss the possibility that my daughter could be with Jesus.

The doctors departed the room leaving us to deal with the information they had just delivered. It did not take much time before Nora and I came into agreement on two things. Though we would still have our emotional highs and lows, we agreed not to ever blame one another and to believe God would perform a miracle with Ariella.

Shortly after the meeting with the doctors, I discussed separately with the resident doctor about the tests they were doing and what they were looking for; I wanted more information. I did not realize that Nora had stayed in the holding room and was standing and raising her hands to God as she looked out the large windows of the room. She spotted a large cemetery across the street from the hospital. She later shared with me that while I was talking with the doctor, she was talking with the Lord. Looking out those windows and seeing the equivalent to death, she cried out to God, "God, please heal Ariella." From a deep place in her heart, she said, "But Lord, if she is to be with you today, I will surrender to that as well." For the first time, she let herself feel all the emotions of this horrific accident. After a few minutes, Nora gathered herself and said, "But for right now, Lord, I am believing you for her healing, I know you can do it."

Nora told me that when she had said that, she felt a release, a lifting, an unexplainable sense of peace. Her experience with the Lord brought a scripture to my mind: "And the peace of God, which passeth all understanding, shall keep your hearts and minds through Christ Jesus" (Philippians 4:7 KJV). The Lord had given Nora a supernatural gift of faith believing for Ariella's healing. Her bold proclamation in conversation with God was matched with an incomprehensible peace. I did not have that kind of boldness or inner peace yet; that took time. I did not get to the place of belief where Nora was for nearly the entire first day. Nora was in the fighting hole with Jesus. I was standing outside the fighting hole looking to Jesus for Ariella's healing, strength for her and our family, and peace.

In the first twenty-four hours, I experienced brokenness, powerlessness, frustration, and anger. Nora maintained her composure and was a great help to me. It took time for me, and it took God's grace and loving-kindness of God, the prayers and prophetic words from the community of faith in the United States and overseas, and our friends and family.

During that first day, we contacted our pastors, family, close friends, and pastors and churches throughout the country. Many of them came in person to support us and pray for Ariella. Many churches held intercessory prayer services for her. We learned later just how much the community of faith had sought God for Ariella's miracle. Churches throughout the world were in their default fighting position praying, prophesying, and holding onto the promises of God for my daughter. Nora took a step of action in her belief for Ariella.

Nora makes small bottles of oil made with lavender and other natural ingredients that we bless and use in prayer. Scripture tells us the enemy comes to steal, kill, and destroy. The adversary was on an assignment, but Nora was as well. She used the oil to anoint the archway of Ariella's room and every doorknob. She prayed for every physician, nurse, family member, and clergy member who would come through the door to be anointed by God, to be filled with faith, and to bring contagious positivity. Nora has a prophetic anointing she has been operating in for more than a decade. She was an active member of her church's prophetic team. I witnessed her on many occasions prophesying to others only to see their miracles later realized. I have seen her speak life and power into the dead places of people in need of hope and healing, and I have seen them blessed and strengthened. Her heroic actions and prophetic voice were critical in these early days.

I had called my parents earlier that morning with the news that our baby had suffered a drowning accident. Three and a half hours later, my parents, James and Karen, along with my sister Kimberly and brother Kristopher arrived from Albany, New York. Nora's sister Yokia and brother Shalom came right away as they lived locally. Nora's older brother, Rodger, came later in the day as well. Our great friends, Matt and Susan Cameron, had taken our children from my son, Jacob, to care for them while we were in the hospital with Ariella. They had grandchildren my children could play with and keep their minds off Ariella. Plus, Aunt Susan could cook a mean spaghetti.

During the first several hours, Nora and I did not comprehend all that was taking place on the outside, but what was happening undoubtedly pressed into God's heart. That evening, we learned that Ariella's condition had not changed much. Shalom shared that when he heard the story on the local news, he had been stunned. He said, "I knew I could not be there right away, so I started to pray. When I prayed, I experienced a sense of peace. I had so much peace when I prayed for Ariella. I knew she was going to be all right. I knew she was fine."

I appreciated his faith-filled reassurance. He stayed for a while until other family reinforcements arrived. Shalom is a hospital nurse and had to report for duty. Nora's sister Yokia remained with us. She is there for everything! Nora and her sister are very close; they shared the births of their children and every other major life event.

When my family arrived, in my logical state of mind, I shared with them what the PICU lead physician had told us. We stood out in the hallway embracing and crying. I shared with them that we believed God would perform a miracle. I asked them to believe with us.

Chapter

3

*Prayers and Prophetic Words
from the Community of Faith*

*The eyes of the LORD are upon the righteous,
and his ears are open unto their cry.*
—Psalm 34:15 KJV

When my parents and siblings walked into Ariella's room, I shared with them the horrific prognosis for Ariella, and they were speechless. Time seems to stand still at moments like those.

My brother Kris later pulled me to the side and said, "Patrick, we can take any part of Ariella no matter what that is. You can take that!" I understood what he was saying, but I wanted a miracle!

As truthful as that sentiment was, I was not even considering his point about having "any" part of Ariella back. I wanted every part of her back. As bizarre as it may sound, I never considered any other condition. My reality rested in two camps—one, she would recover completely, or two—she was going to be with Jesus.

Looking back at it now, I see how my brother expressed those encouraging words of hope. When Kris was fifteen, he dove into a pool and broke his neck. He lay paralyzed for nine months with a prognosis of never walking again. He underwent a difficult surgery, and a few months later, he came to stay with me in Camp Pendleton, California. My fellow Marines and I trained that young man intensely. Kris not only walks today; he is also a serious fitness nut who is married and has a beautiful family. He had experienced a miracle. Kris was speaking to me from a place of experience and understanding tragedy. Yet that moment, I could not consider any other outcomes; they simply did not register with me.

My family continued to take turns to see Ariella, and *quiet* is the only word I can use to describe their reaction. Ariella had wires connected all over her head. She was being helped to breathe. She was heavily sedated and seemingly lifeless. My mother, Karen, a nurse, was reading charts, inspecting the lines and connections, and observing the nurses' and the physicians' efforts. They visited for a while. We agreed that they would get the kids from Matt and Susan and care for them at our home. Jacob, Ethan, and Gianna still had to be reeling from what they had experienced that morning and were certainly worried about their baby sister. They had witnessed Nora doing CPR, my shouting out orders, and the first responders and their efforts to resuscitate Ariella. The kids were still highly emotional and concerned. We believed the familiar faces of Noni and Popi—their grandma and grandpa—would help Ethan and Gianna get their minds on something else. They could have a nice dinner and catch up. This was a healthy distraction. So they left the hospital after a few hours and went to get the kids.

What followed their departure was difficult. As you can imagine, an event like that brought Child Protective Services (CPS) and local sheriff's investigators into the situation. A CPS staffer asked to meet Nora and me to discuss what had happened to Ariella. It was difficult to relive the horror of that morning with them. It was a surreal experience as it seemed we had arrived at the hospital just moments earlier. We shared with the investigators and the CPS social worker exactly what had happened. All the authorities were professional and understanding. We were transparent, and the case would be later closed.

Regarding safety, Nora and I had child locks and gates throughout our home, but when you think you have things in place, you discover there's more to do. Nora and I knew CPR, and I learned from this experience that families must know CPR including infant CPR to continually improve child safety at home. I had always known and practiced this, but families must have meetings to discuss emergency plans for fires and other incidents such as break-ins or intruders. They must discuss where they should meet inside and outside the house. Being vigilant about home safety is critical and can save lives. There can never be too much time dedicated to it. The meeting with the sheriff and the social worker ended, and we returned to Ariella's side.

That evening, calls and texts came in with heartfelt words of compassion and support. I had spoken to our pastor, Dom Renault, in Rochester, and my longtime pastor, John Marshall, in Virginia. Their compassion, words of hope, and prayers were so welcome. When you are inside the hospital with your child experiencing this, you are in a bubble. Nora and I were unaware of the numerous efforts to pray for Ariella. Prayer chains were developing, and connections of the church were being made as the news of Ariella reached throughout the United States and overseas. In Rochester, every news station was covering Ariella's story, and the local community of faith was ignited in praying for Ariella. Psalm 34:15 was in motion—God's people were crying out on behalf of Ariella.

Pastor Dom came quickly, and as he talked with Nora and me, he also quietly listened to us. He focused on the dream I had had that morning and reminded me and Nora that God had sent that dream to prepare us for this time. As Pastor Dom has been in the past, he was impressed with my wife's strength and faith. He encouraged me to maintain hope and stand on that dream, on the authority in Christ, and on my words "No you are not!"

He felt strongly that God had given me that dream to anchor Nora and me. Pastor Dom prayed with Ariella and us. He informed us that the entire church would be lifting Ariella up now and each day moving forward. I walked him out, and he embraced me with a father's love.

During this first day, most people were being respectful by not coming to the hospital, and we understood and appreciated that. That would change in the days to come. And its orchestration and timing could only have been God.

Ariella remained supported by the medical equipment; her condition had not changed. She remained sedated and was on a respirator and ventilator. She was being intravenously fed, and the EEG was monitoring her brain activity. It was a long evening of being with our daughter. I spent some time reading to Nora texts and emails from loved ones. One of the emails I received was from Helen, a woman who attended our church, Bethel Christian Fellowship in Rochester. Nora served on the same prophetic team with Helen in years past. I do not mean at all to diminish the other messages of encouragement we received, but her email stood out. It was a prophetic word that was life changing for Nora and me and I am convinced for Ariella: "Ariella's name means 'Lioness of the Lord.'"

Nora and I knew this as it was one reason we had named her Ariella. Helen's words that followed leaped off the screen and began to stir up my faith. I had one leg over the sandbags and was climbing into the fighting position of belief.

Helen emailed, "Ariella is a Lioness of the Lord, and though Satan has made this attack on her, that will not stand as the Lord is walking with her. She will be a witness and boldly proclaim God to the world ... Ariella will have no lasting effects from this incident, and she will be made whole without any evidence of trauma!"

How specific was this prophetic word? Pretty specific!

Her words were filled with a boldness and a confidence I had not yet achieved. Her words had the same confidence that Pastor Marshall's words had had earlier. The words were specific—no gray area, nothing ambiguous.

Helen wrote, "Perform this prayer over Ariella and do it often." We quickly moved to read and pray those prayers and promises over our daughter. It had to look and sound bizarre to those in the room. We got into a flow; I read Helen's words to Nora, and we prayed them over Ariella. Nora and I filled the room with prayer, and for the first moment I can recall, I believed God would perform a miracle. Psalm 34:15 describes God's people in tears, crying, prophesying, praying, and seeking the Lord's eyes for healing. This psalm was being lived out real time in Ariella's room, and God was being attentive to us.

The hospital staff planned for Nora and me to stay in the Ronald McDonald house, which was above the PICU. They recommended we take a few hours to shower and sleep if possible. They would get us immediately if there were any changes. After we held, kissed, and talked with Ariella, Nora and I agreed that getting some rest for a few hours was necessary. The nurses saw that we were not comfortable leaving; every moment mattered so deeply. They reassured us again that Ariella would be monitored closely and that they would call us if anything changed.

It was late into the night; Nora and I planned to return at the next shift change early in the morning. Shift changes were so important. We got to hear the turnover reports on Ariella's case from doctor and staff to the next team. Nora and I wanted to glean any information from those briefs in real time to better understand Ariella's condition and progress.

Nora and I went upstairs to the Ronald McDonald House, and we saw several families there experiencing crises like ours. While in the common area, I gathered a couple waters and snacks for Nora, and I began to speak with a father who shared he was losing his son. He said that his son was fighting but that the prognosis was poor. That floor was filled with despair and anxiety; families were in agony as were we.

I returned to our room. Nora was lying down, and I began to pray loudly. I was crying out to God pleading with Him to heal my daughter, and I began angrily to denounce the work of Satan and his demons in their efforts against Ariella. At some point, I was praying and crying out so loudly that the staff came to check on us and asked if I could keep it down. I apologized and agreed to be quieter. But a battle was going on in me where faith and fear met, and all that I had was God's truth and His Word, which stood in stark contrast to the physicians' reports. A war was raging between what my flesh was hearing and the voice of truth in me. I had to direct my thoughts and words toward God's Word. I had to fight from the position of belief. I knew God could do supernatural works despite everything I had seen and heard.

Nora and I continued to pray quietly as we consoled one another; she remained strong in her faith. Her words and actions matched her demeanor, and she never wavered. We attempted to get some rest and planned to wake early to get back downstairs to Ariella and listen to that second-day shift change.

As we went into the evening of that first night in the hospital, Ariella's condition still had not changed. We hoped for some good news on the second day.

Chapter

4

The Second Day (August 20–21)

You are the God who performs miracles; you display your power among the peoples.
—Psalm 77:14 KJV

Nora and I made it down to Ariella's room the second day and listened intently to the shift-change brief. We learned that routine tests had returned negative, and that was good news. We were ecstatic with every good test result no matter how insignificant.

We welcomed the insight of the new physician and her treatment plan for the day. That is when Dr. Judy McMann became Ariella's primary physician while in PICU as far as Nora and I were concerned. We instantly connected with her and valued her expertise and care for Ariella. She said Ariella had had a fever throughout the night, which had required additional medication. She indicated that she considered Ariella's CT (computerized tomography) scan and EEG to be grossly abnormal: "The evidence and pattern observed sufficiently shows Ariella as having severe encephalopathy"; she was referring to a brain disease that altered function. I later learned that meant her brain had been severely damaged by a toxin or agent to an unknown extent. There was not much to cling to in that update. Our greatest takeaway was Ariella had not had any additional seizures throughout the night, and that was a major positive development. Ariella was still entirely dependent on the machines. Despite not having much good news with Ariella, day two offered some encouragement in hearing about the support from others.

Nora and I did not fully understand the buzz Ariella's story was getting at that point, but God was beginning to display His power. Ariella's story was bringing so many people together seeking God for the miraculous. We could not appreciate it as we were going through it, but there was great interest in Ariella's story, and we learned more as the hours went by.

On this second day, the visitors who came shared with us all that was going on. Interviews were taking place with the amazing first responders, the volunteer first responders, and our neighbors Pam and Charles, Jim and Cathleen, and Nancy. Many of them were interviewed by news stations to share what they did and what they knew, and they offered their prayers for Ariella. Churches were praying for her and holding services for her, and Ariella's story was racing through social media. We learned that Pam, Cathleen, and Nancy had brought over food for our children and extended family who had arrived from out of town. The Town of Chili stepped in; its people offered their assistance, and several contractors offered to close the pool. The kindness and support they extended was moving, and it meant a great deal to Nora and me while we were with Ariella. We knew our children were worried and hurting also, so having such strong family and community support was so important.

Considering the news we received from the doctor, we had nothing we could tell our children. We facetimed with Jacob, Ethan, and Gianna hoping that seeing our faces would ease their anxiety. Nora and I asked them to be hopeful, to believe. We reassured them Ariella was going to be okay. We told them this was the stand we were taking. I reminded them, "We know and believe God can do anything." All things considered, the kids sounded okay.

My aunts Maureen and Patty arrived from Albany, and as nearly everyone was, they were moved to tears when they saw Ariella. I have found that in these times, particularly when a parent is dealing with the possible loss of a child, no words can adequately address the pain and heartache they feel. I had been in that position before when telling a Marine's dad and mom that he had been killed in action. I witnessed their shock and disbelief and tried to answer their questions as they were trying to make sense of their loss.

I experienced it again when a young couple, members of my church I pastored in Japan, had lost their infant. I felt completely inadequate; I doubted any words in the sermon I preached would help them. I learned through that experience that it was more about just being present. Inadequate words to inconsolable parents describe these two instances well. My aunts were present with us that day. Nora and I were praying not to ever hear news like those parents had.

On day two, more people came to be present and pray in addition to our pastor, family, and friends. My seminary faculty came in full force. Reverend Dan Callahan, the president of Northeastern Seminary, came and spoke powerful words over Ariella and prayed with us. Professors Neal Gerald and

Renee Lederman arrived and spent time with Nora and me. A supernatural spiritual momentum was developing, and I was witnessing it firsthand.

Pastor Dom came back and shared words of encouragement and exhortation with us. He looked at Ariella and said, "God raising up Ariella is going to be a manifestation of what Christ did two thousand years ago on the cross. God's Word tells us that by His stripes we are healed." His words and presence gave us great comfort. His conviction was palpable. One common observation regarding all of them was that they all had taken their fighting position of believing.

Jose Rosas, a great friend and seminary classmate in my cohort, the 34th, arrived. I met him in the hallway outside the PICU, and we spent time together. I tried to keep it together; after all, I was supposed to be his mentor. But when he reached out to hug me, I sank into his six-five frame and cried uncontrollably. The immensity of the ordeal had been overwhelming. Jose brought us food. He is that person you know who wants to be whatever you need in a crisis. He suggested that Nora or I should go home, check on the kids, and get some clothes. Nora and I discussed it and agreed I would go and be right back.

Jose brought me home, where my entire family and the kids greeted me. The news crews there were respectful. The kids were still eating the food the neighbors had brought over. Of course, my mom with her nervous energy had cleaned the whole house, and I got a debrief from my dad and brother on the efforts made to close the pool. My dad said that several reporters had requested updates or comments but that he had declined them. He said many friends had stopped by to check on Ariella, and I saw he was moved by those supporting Ariella and our family. I spent some time with the kids, and they seemed to be distracted in a good way with Noni, Popi, and their aunts and uncles. I grabbed clothes for Nora and me and made my way back to the hospital.

When I returned, I gave Nora her clothes and encouraged her to get some rest as I sat with Ariella. Nora went upstairs to rest, shower, and change. Since Ariella was very little, I always sang songs to her—"Amazing Grace," "Jesus Loves Me," "I Love You and You Love Me"—the list goes on and on. I spent much of the evening singing to her our hits in hopes she would hear me and wake up. I could not get through many of the songs very well.

Ariella and I would make one-minute videos of her whether she was doing something fun or just sitting with me in the recliner; she loved seeing herself on the phone videos. Earlier on the morning she fell into the pool, I took a video of her walking across her room as I talked with her; she said her baby talk and kept it moving. I played some of our videos so she could hear all our antics. While I was with her, nurses checked on her often. I can only imagine what they were thinking. With agonizing heartache, I told Ariella how sorry I was for this having happened to her. I told her how incredibly strong she was being and that Daddy needed her to keep fighting.

Ariella had been a fighter from birth. She had been a breech baby; the first thing I saw when Ariella was born was her rear end. I'm not sure what she was trying to say to the world or to me then, but it has always matched her personality. After a minute or so, I saw her right foot, and then her left, and then her beautiful face. They placed a little yellow hat on her and wrapped her in a blue-striped blanket. To Nora's dismay, I videotaped the entire experience; that was Ariella's first video we made together. She was moving around, making faces, and generally unhappy with all the nurses. The second day she was in the hospital after her accident was a far cry from that incredible memory; she was lying motionless and fighting for her life.

Nora walked in when I was singing one of my classics to Ariella; she saw I had been crying.

She asked, "Has anyone been by?"

"No, a few nurse visits but not any updates."

Nora asked if I wanted something to drink. We were living off those cranberry drinks they had in the refrigerator for the families. She said, "I'll get you one and stop by to talk with the staff to get an update."

"Thanks, honey. That'll be good."

Nora returned accompanied by the night-shift physician who shared with us that the first seventy-two hours continued to be the most crucial and that if the swelling on her brain did not stop, she would not make it. Everything they were seeing remained the same. The sedation and machines were keeping her alive; they could not predict anything. Hearing these words over and over was extremely difficult.

The doctor said, "The next hurdle for Ariella to cross is breathing above the ventilator."

She explained to us that they would be looking for Ariella to take on her breathing more and that if she did, they would wean her from the ventilator and it would do less work. Ariella had to achieve a milestone of breathing "above" the ventilator at approximately 80 percent for it to be turned off and for Ariella to take over.

Chapter

5

*The Third Day
(August 21–22)*

*When any one heareth the word of the kingdom, and
understandeth it not, then cometh the wicked one,
and catcheth away that which was sown in his heart.
This is he which received seed by the way side.*
—Mark 13:19 KJV

I t was Sunday, a day we ordinarily would be going to church
in the morning and out to lunch as was our family custom.
Ariella had made it through the night, and the physicians
informed us that her liver tests had improved—great news.

The physicians were waiting to see Ariella's responses to adjustments they had made throughout the evening.

Nora and I spent the morning with Ariella talking with her, singing to her, and holding her hand. Nora played songs for Ariella on her cell phone, songs Ariella knew. Looking back, I realize Nora believed Ariella would hear the songs and wake up. In that moment of watching my wife with Ariella, I took some comfort in knowing that Jesus had been with Ariella the entire time talking with her and that she was not experiencing pain; she was peacefully wrapped up in His love. We spent the morning asking God to heal her and asking Ariella to hear us and wake up.

Later that morning, I logged onto my church's website on my phone to see if we could listen to our pastor's sermon. Nora and I needed some encouragement, and hearing the preached Word of God would be a welcomed alternative to most of the news we had been hearing. I pulled up the site and opened the message, which was about to stream live. Pastor Dom's sermon was about "Understanding Seed" (Mark 13:19) and how as Christian believers, we must not allow the enemy, Satan, to take from us the Word of God we have received and believed. I was intrigued by the message and understood his instructions and encouragement in this area.

Then he began to talk about Ariella. "Nora and Patrick were given a dream in advance as a seed, as an anchor to hold onto during this storm of hearing 'facts' of severe brain damage. But these facts are not the truth."

His words were confirming things I felt in my spirit, words of incredible comfort.

He declared, "Ariella is in Jesus, and Jesus is in her."

Pastor Dom taught that it was important to understand the Word of God as a seed. It was noticeable on the broadcast that his visits with Ariella had affected him. He exclaimed, "After fifty years in ministry, I will no longer accept less than above-average results." Even today, I wonder what that statement meant. What does it mean to you? Are we accepting less than average results? For me, his statement spoke to our God-given gift to believe in a way that seems illogical to many, but because of the Word of God, we are able to remain in the position of believing. Not believing is an act on our part of surrendering the Word of God. When we choose not to believe, all God's promises and the miraculous are certain to be stolen from us. At a minimum, it leaves us hopeless.

Through his sermon, Pastor Dom warned us not to let the seed be choked out or stolen from us. His sermon struck a chord in me. This was a time to dig in deeper with my wife, to press into God more deeply for Ariella, and to trust and know God was capable of healing Ariella.

Pastor Dom led the church at the end of the service in an anointed prayer for Ariella. He shared words similar but slightly different when he had visited and prayed with her the day before. In his sermon, he prayed, "Lord, we declare the healing you purchased two thousand years ago will be made in her body, a specific seed sown, for she shall live and not die and will proclaim the Word of the Lord!" The response Nora and I had after hearing this sermon and Pastor Dom's words was, "Yes! Believing is all we have. There's no other position to take." Over and over, we heard words of brain damage and death, but along with them came words of healing and life. Given those two choices, why would we in any way entertain the death of our daughter?

After I listened to Pastor Dom's sermon, I reflected on all the prayers, the incredible number of visitors, clergy, community, texts, emails, and the outpouring of compassion that came our way; a spiritual tidal wave. During the day, I learned that churches in New York, Virginia, North Carolina, South Carolina, Louisiana, and even Japan were bombarding heaven with petitions for Ariella's miracle. So many were believing for Ariella's miracle, and they would continue to visit Ariella and declare the same.

That evening, my best friend, Matt Cameron, who has experienced life with me through many difficult trials, visited Ariella. Matt and I worked in men's ministry together for many years. In 2009, I desired to have a men's ministry that provided a place where men could be transparent, talk about difficult issues, and receive accountability and friendship. Matt was there from the beginning. In some ways, the ministry was created out of necessity to be a place where I could express my heart. Matt and I would hold monthly, sometimes biweekly meetings, and men would come. We would eat, fellowship, and share our hearts. After all, how well do we truly know the other men in the congregation we belong to? I mean *really* know them—to hear their stories, to be listened to, and to be understood? As a man who has experienced difficulties, I selfishly enjoyed the fellowship as its transparent and honest discussion helped heal my heart. Matt and I made ourselves available to God to help men, and God always seems to open a door and send a man. God would do this in such curious ways.

A few months before Ariella's accident, I went into the backyard to cut my lawn and saw my neighbor Paul, who was eighty-three and had lost his wife just a few weeks earlier. He was a hard-working man; he was outside cutting wood. I made my way over to talk with him. We sat on two logs he had just cut. We made some small talk, and then he began to share his heart with me. He said, "I lived a full life." He had had a wonderful wife and marriage—kids and grandkids. He had made a good living. Paul knew I had been in the Marines, and he told me that many years ago, he had installed an old tank in front of the Marine Headquarters building with a crane at the local Marine Corps unit where I served. I saw he took great pride in that, and he expressed how hard it had been to accomplish the task.

His voice changed when he talked about his wife. He said, "I don't know how to live without her."

Paul was a strong man, a family man, proud of his life and family, and was well known in the community. He told me he had a lot of stuff in the house. He described how things were going to be so different with his wife gone. He used to invite my sons over to his house, and he showed them his vintage weapons he had in the garage. He and I would always make small talk over the years, and I always attributed his distance as the way of that special generation of World War II vets— few words but major action. That day was different. He shared his heart with me as his eyes welled up with tears. I took it all in as an incredible honor that he would share a difficult part of his life with me. God was at work in our hearts.

Afterward, he said, "Hey, let's get back to work." And we returned to our chores.

Paul died a few months later. The ministry Matt and I had been led to start was for all the Pauls who lived every day working hard, raising families, and holding onto simple values—men with incredible stories to tell.

Matt talked with us for a while as he looked on Ariella. While we were talking, my brother-in-law Rodger, a man full of faith, came to visit Ariella. He must have figured I could use some coffee; he invited me to go to the cafeteria. Matt said that he would stay with Nora and Ariella and that we should get us all some coffee.

"Okay, let's go," I told Rodger.

He and I sat in the cafeteria; he talked about how powerful and loving God was. He said he felt strongly that God was on top of Ariella's situation. "When I heard the news," he said, "I knew God was up to something. I knew He'd do something miraculous." He spoke with an assurance and from a place of confidence, and I attempted to grab hold of the hope he spoke of. He believed. He helped me stand firm in my belief. I needed that. I was grateful for his encouragement and talk. It was as if he knew I needed to focus on something else even if just for a moment. He and I made small talk catching up on the kids and work before we made our way back to Ariella's room.

Rodger stood with Matt, Nora, and me and said, "Guys, this is all over the news. This is everywhere. God's going to do a miracle in Ariella for all the world to see." His faith moved us.

Believing is contagious. Relying on others' faith increases my own faith. With every prayer and prophetic word, my belief is emboldened. Rodger hugged us; he had to get home to his family.

Matt stood with his hands coupled in front of him. He was a warrior with an incredible life to share. He shared with men and women who needed to hear his story of God's grace, his personal triumph, and what God was doing in the world today. He was a watchman. He believed. Matt was passionate and walked with the Holy Spirit so strongly that if you didn't pay attention, you might miss the message for your life.

Matt asked to pray with Ariella; God filled the room with His presence—a sweet but powerful rush of life came into the room. He asked God to heal Ariella and cause her to live. He spoke to Ariella, to her body, and he laid hands on her. The presence of God was rich. Matt finished praying and asked Nora and me, "Did you feel that?"

"Yes, yes!" we responded in unison.

An incredible lifting had occurred, and we were encouraged by Matt's love and prayer of authority. Matt knew who he was in God. That moment could not have been any different. He would be there for my family and me in any battle. His heart burned so passionately, his mind was so sharp, and his spiritual IQ was so off the charts in the prophetic sense and in the times in which we lived that I could not have chosen a better warrior to go to battle with.

It was getting into the evening. Matt embraced Nora and me. I walked him out.

When I returned to Nora and Ariella, Nora was just looking at her. I had read and heard that when couples go through these kinds of devastating circumstances, their marriages just don't survive. Nora and I wanted to be different. We agreed from the beginning that that would not be us. It was no one's fault; it had just happened. Ariella was so curious and energetic, and she moved so quickly that short of being right there with her every second, that kind of accident could happen.

We shared with each other how powerful Matt's visit was and how grateful we were for his words. From the moment Nora snatched Ariella out of the pool until that very moment in her room, God had made Himself present in our pain. I believe that when He saw me struggle, He sent another person, another word, another message, another prayer, another sermon; whatever I needed to hear at times like that between all the beeping and nurses and doctors walking in and out was given. There are a lot of words unspoken; for me, the quiet was a way to cope, take a breather from the roller-coaster we were on, and hear and read God's Word and promises.

Several hours later, I received a text from my friend Matt, who had left earlier. He said, "Ariella shall live, and she shall be raised up on the third day."

He shared with me his thought about that text before he had sent it. He realized the difficulty of taking the position of believing faced with this tragedy. He shared that he had felt compelled by God and the Holy Spirit to send it to Nora and me—not to question it but to boldly profess what he believed. His text took me by surprise. I called Matt, and he said it was not just a prophetic word; he said, "I had such an assurance that I knew it to be true."

At every turn, the Lord was providing encouraging words. I thanked Matt for listening to the Holy Spirit and for sending us this incredible word. After wrapping up our call, I shared it with Nora, and she was encouraged to hear Matt's bold words. She recalled that Matt had prayed for Ariella at her bedside and that with tears in his eyes had asked to pray for her. It was different in that many of those who had prayed for Ariella had us draw closer, but that Matt had not. Obviously, we were united with him in his prayer, but there was an authority present, and God came into the room. His was a unique and life-giving blessing at the right time.

The evening went on. Nora and I were very tired and emotionally drained. We spent the night talking with Ariella, loving on her, and encouraging each other. I was amazed at my wife's strength and faith throughout this ordeal. I knew that men were to be the rock and possess faith in every circumstance and every trial, but it was Nora who had that supernatural faith for our baby. I witnessed what the true gift of faith looks like up close and personal. In faith, we began to speak about the days that lay ahead for Ariella and the amazing testimony she would have regarding God's grace toward her.

As we looked on her, I commented, "She's talking and walking with Jesus right now. He has her, and she's okay." Some might say this was what parents say when all hope is lost, but I had not lost all hope. I was comforted by the Word of God, which tells us He cares for children in a unique way. I sensed throughout this time that Ariella was being comforted. Logic cannot speak to what I am describing because it moves us away from the supernatural. If we rely too much on the natural, only what we can see, we miss the opportunity for the miraculous to occur in our lives. I believe Jesus was weeping with us; He shared in the pain Nora and I were feeling.

Around eight that night, a nurse made some adjustments to Ariella and double-checked all her equipment. She made some small talk, but then, she must have felt comfortable to share more than that with us. She said, "My father is a pastor at Zion Fellowship in Canandaigua, New York, about twenty-five minutes south of Rochester, and he and the entire congregation are praying for Ariella." She shared that it was such a blessing for her to be a nurse, to share her faith, and to speak words of faith in the presence of Ariella, Nora, me, and other believers. She expressed how life-giving it was to have the opportunity to share and join in on the spiritual collaboration of believers petitioning God for a miracle.

Up to then, no one on the staff had shared his or her faith with us, but she wanted us to know she was believing too. It caught me off guard, but I counted it as another whisper from God. She said she would be praying for Ariella, and she wished us a good evening and some rest. God continued to send people who were in the fighting position of believing.

It was getting late. Nora and I looked up and saw a beautiful couple from our church walk in the room. Victor and Darla Garcia are pillars of the ministry. Victor is the church prophet. Darla had been the connection between my family and others during that time; she was the conduit who made all the communication possible. She had been sending texts and relaying prayers and emails to me for the previous twenty-four hours. She had notified Pastor Dom. She was a main anchor to the outside and all the synergy that was developing in the church and community. Ironically, she had been the photographer for our wedding.

They visited for a while, and Victor asked if he could pray for Ariella, and of course, Nora and I welcomed that. Victor prayed fervently, and in the middle of that prayer, he declared, "Ariella will live—she is already healed!" Nora and I did not know how great their faith was until he and his wife shared more.

In their belief, they had bought an outfit for my baby Ariella to wear out of the hospital. They had an unwavering sense of peace as they shopped for an outfit believing that God was restoring Ariella. This was an incredible example of action meeting faith, of believing God for the miracle, and of a belief in actions as if they were already done. Victor and Darla were in the fighting position of believing; they had purchased spiritual weapons and begun to take aim at the enemy.

They hugged us, and we agreed to remain in touch. They left. I again stood in awe of what God was saying through numerous people many of whom did not know one another. It was as if God were trying to comfort Nora and me and wanting to establish and show His glory and power in and through Ariella to all involved. And He was doing it over and over.

Nora and I spoke to the night-shift physician, and based on the plan for the evening, Nora and I decided to go upstairs to the Ronald McDonald house room, shower, and get some rest if that was possible. Again, the physician and nurses said they would get us if they had any news. Nora and I made the long walk to the elevator and went up to our room. We reviewed all the information we had learned from the doctors and discussed all the amazing prayers and prophetic words of life and faith. There was an amazing collective voice of the church—not just our church but also the Christian church that was united in prayer for Ariella's full recovery. Nora and I agreed we had never seen anything like that. We got some snacks from the common area and tried to get a couple of hours' sleep.

Chapter

6

The Fourth Day (August 22–23)

For we live by faith, not by sight.
2 Corinthians 5:7 NIV

This nightmare started with a dream and an evil presence threatening to take my daughter. Just before waking up the next morning at the Ronald McDonald House, I had a second dream. In it, I was in the hospital lobby and saw a masked man in all black with a machine-gun coming through the double doors that opened automatically. I ran at him and tackled him, took the weapon from him, fought with him, and dragged him out.

Then I woke up. God was speaking to me; He was ensuring I remained in the fighting position of believing. It is a hard position to hold; it has enemies and assignments. We must engage in the spiritual warfare because whether we like it or not, we are in it. Taking authority and holding the fighting position of believing is battle. Was another attack coming, or was the attacker dragged out the door for good? Had the church, the community, family, friends, clergy, prophets, Nora, and I held the position and received the grace of God's miraculous works?

I shared the dream with Nora right away; we went down to Ariella's floor and asked for an update at the nurses' station. They were hesitant to share specifics; they said they would have the resident physician see us. That happened around 5:30 a.m.; the doctor told us that they had been pleasantly shocked to have seen that Ariella's liver was improving and that all other test results were coming back with good results. She did not give any false hope or a lofty prognosis; she said only that this was good. The plan was to begin weaning her off sedation. It was a waiting game for Dr. McMann and the oncoming shift.

We were grateful for the glimmer of good news; I called my family. My father, mother, sister, and brother came to the hospital and sat with us. Nora and I spent the better part of the morning talking and singing to Ariella. I cannot explain fully what I was seeing, but the doctors and nurses all had an undeniable sense of urgency and excitement. Paraphrasing Hebrews 11:1b, "Through faith, an assurance was occurring in what I could not see." I suggest they had seen things in Ariella that changed their outward demeanor. Nora and I picked up on their smiles; many of the staff seemed outwardly optimistic though they kept their cards close.

Out of nowhere, my mom said, "There's been a change in this room."

"Mom, what do you mean?" I asked.

"There's something going on here. Ariella's going to be fine."

I was astonished with the impact God was having on her. My mom loves and believes in God, but to hear her make that kind of proclamation was highly unusual.

Nora and I looked forward to hearing Dr. McMann's plan of action. We attended the morning shift change, which was right outside our doorway. Dr. McMann said they were slowly reducing the medications and her sedation to allow her to wake up. She shared with the staff their responsibilities and functions. What was usually a ten-minute brief felt like an hour. The words she said next will never leave my mind, and they came out of nowhere: "It is my expectation that when Ariella wakes up, she will be her normal self." I exclaimed, "Her normal self?"

Nora and I could barely contain ourselves. We embraced and were filled with joy although we still had some way to go. Dr. McMann and her team monitored Ariella closely and took it a step at a time. As Ariella was weaned off sedation, the staff watched her ability to take over her breathing. They extubated her, and Ariella was able to breathe 80 percent above the ventilator—she was doing the majority of the work. Nora and I talked softly to Ariella. We wanted to reassure her that Daddy and Mommy were with her and that she was okay. There were still nerves and tears, but everyone in the room was optimistic. My father, James, could not stay still; he spent time pacing and walking around the hospital. My mom, Karen, brother Kris, and sister Kimberly were trying to keep Nora and me engaged in conversation, but it inevitably came back to Ariella. What seemed like hours took only a few minutes. Nora and I had stepped out of the room to take a lap around the PICU. As we made our way around, Kris came running out of the room and said, "Pat, she made eye contact with me!"

I excitedly asked, "What do you mean?"

"She scanned the room, and I was standing right over her, and she locked right onto me. She looked at me intentionally! She was looking at the nurses and then locked eyes with me again!"

He was overwhelmed and began to weep as he hugged me.

Nora and I ran into Ariella's room; nurses and doctors gathered around her. The word had gotten to the larger team, and many of them were caring for her. Amazingly, our Ariella did not like the little air hose in her nose and was trying to take it out; the nurses had to restrain her arms to ensure she left it alone. It seemed as busy as when they had rushed her into the ER, but this time, it was calmer and more deliberate.

My father returned; he was known for his strength, but even he was visibly moved. "I can't believe she's awake. I can't believe it."

Astonished, he shook my hand and hugged Nora and me with a grateful heart. He walked out of the room overtaken by his emotions. God was displaying His miraculous works for us to see.

Nora and I looked into her eyes, held her hands, and caressed her face. She was looking around the room. She was uncomfortable, but it appeared to me she did have a sense of her surroundings. The medical staff wanted to allow her to wake up fully.

Slowly, Ariella became more alert. The doctors and nurses performed several tests each of which came back with favorable results. The medical staff started saying what was on their minds; they were smiling and were enjoying their work.

As the medications wore completely off, Ariella rapidly regained her neurological function. Dr. McMann shared with us that she was lining up the necessary specialists to conduct a complete assessment, which would take several hours. They kept the EEG on her to continue to monitor her brain activity. We talked with her, and she began to talk her baby talk as Nora and I comforted her.

Nora asked the nurses, "Can I hold her?"

The staff made some adjustments to the wires connected to her head as Nora sat in the chair next to the bed. I will never forget that moment when Mommy held Ariella in her arms. My baby girl was looking around at all the people and blinking lights. She was clearly hearing the beeping sounds. Our baby girl was alive and alert to her surroundings. After a short few hours, Ariella was standing on the bed with Mommy supporting her. In that incredible moment, Ariella looked like the lioness of the Lord. I took a picture of her as she was standing on her own two feet. Despite all she had been through, she stood there with a look of determination. We were witnesses to Ariella's miracle!

She was first evaluated by neurology; they reported, "Found no residual deficits and did not see an indication for scheduled follow-up at this time." She was evaluated by speech pathology and passed their assessment with no necessity for follow-up. She was evaluated by the nutritionist, who determined Ariella had no limitations. The speech therapist and nutritionist brought Ariella pudding, juice, and crackers, which Ariella eagerly consumed. She passed with flying colors. In fairness to the medical staff, Ariella had a head start earlier in the day; she had been able to let us know she was ready.

Several hours earlier, Ariella's face had expressed sadness, which in Nora's mind had always meant she wanted a bottle. Ariella loved having her bottle for comfort as well as milk. Before this accident, it was one of her most precious joys. Nora asked the nurses if they could bring her a bottle, and Ariella's eyes lit up—her demeanor changed dramatically. There was a joyful twinkle in her eyes! The pudding, crackers, and juice afterward were the icing on the cake.

Several hours later, Ariella was evaluated by physical therapy, and she walked twelve feet. She could sit upright in a seat ring and exhibit the purposeful movements they needed to see. The physical therapist said, "Ariella's doing just fine. We won't need to follow up with her."

One PICU physician's note read, "She hugged her mom, and when she did so, she patted her mom on the back." As I write that, I am moved to tears and my heart is warmed. Ariella was consoling Mom. It was as if she were saying, "I'm all right, Mommy. It's going to be okay."

Dr. Ryan, the ER physician who cared for Ariella when she was first admitted into the ER, had gotten word of Ariella's miraculous recovery. When he walked in, he smiled and stared at her. He shared with us that when he heard the news, he decided he had to see her himself. He stood speechless for several moments.

He smiled at Nora and me and said, "I'm so happy for you. It's unbelievable! It's a remarkable and quick recovery from the little girl I saw just a few days ago." He told us again how happy he was for us and wished us well.

A flood of people wanted to see Ariella. Numerous doctors and nurses who were attending Ariella came to see her during their shifts; she had affected them all, and they wanted to see what God had done for her. The whole hospital was abuzz with word of Ariella's recovery.

Medical staff from other departments stopped by to express their joy and ask, "Can we see the miracle baby? I heard what happened, and I cannot believe it. You know she's a miracle baby?" What God was doing amazed me. Through other people, even strangers, He was telling us what He did. He was telling us He still answered prayers and performed miracles.

A short while later, the resident, Dr. Emily May, who had been with the original lead physician on the first day in the PICU, walked in. She had been there when we were informed that Ariella would never be the same again or might not survive. Dr. May's and Nora's eyes locked; she felt connected to her in a meaningful way. Throughout this experience,

Nora and Dr. May had numerous conversations, and she had patiently answered our questions. She was compassionate and warm to my wife. Emotionally and with a grateful heart, Nora gently reminded her of their exchange that first day. Nora softly asked, "Do you remember?"

Dr. May recalled Nora proclaiming, "No, I cannot accept that. This is not God's plan for Ariella's life. No. I am sorry, but I cannot accept that."

Dr. May smiled and replied, "Yes, I am amazed. It is so good."

Dr. May remained with Dr. McMann throughout and observed Ariella's journey from beginning to end. She remained with Ariella that day as well. She and Nora talked about how this kind of scenario often and sadly went in the other direction. Dr. May gave us well wishes and went to attend to her other duties.

Nora had made her way out of the room to get drinks, and when she was returning, the receptionist at the PICU desk hesitantly asked Nora, "Are you the miracle baby's mother?"

Nora replied, "Yes I am."

"My family and I have been following the news of Ariella, and it was such an encouragement to see how God stepped in. So many in our community have seen it. It's so wonderful."

Nora thanked her for her kind words and said, "God is amazing. Ariella's story is touching people. God is up to something. He's awesome. Thank you for praying for our daughter."

As the room calmed down and Ariella rested, Nora and I spoke about the miracle God had performed and the reports we heard from others. We were rejoicing. We took note that in Ariella's miracle, in God delivering our baby girl, the mouth of the enemy of our souls was closed. Please understand this is not about physicians giving their professional opinions. The staff who cared for her were beyond amazing and world class. What I am speaking about is the voice of our accuser—the voice that was there to kill our baby, the voice that was there to take her life that fateful day. The destroyer that attempted to speak death over her and kill her was silenced and was not present when God placed His mighty works on display for all to see. When we take the fighting position of believing and declaring the Word of God, the enemy flees.

In all these special moments and after hearing numerous people refer to Ariella's recovery and healing as a miracle, I was not considering writing Ariella's story; we were just taking her dramatic recovery in. Nora and I were still dealing with the first day our baby was returned to us. Writing a book was the last thing on my mind. Only after careful consideration and after nearly two years had passed would the pressing of the Holy Spirit change that.

As the great news continued to come with each medical and specialist test, I knew I had to tell everyone who took part in the original prayer chains, emails, and texts the great news. I made a mass email and text notifying anyone who was involved these last several days. I told them simply what God had done—He had healed our little girl!

Chapter

7

The Fifth Day
(August 23–24)

*Now faith is the substance of things hoped
for, the evidence of things not seen.*
Hebrews 11:1 (KJV)

The next twenty-four hours were taken up with observation, monitoring, and ensuring Ariella did not experience any complications. Some of my family had to return to their lives. My father and brother departed. My mom and sister remained to help with our children at home and to support Nora and me.

Dr. McMann told us, "If all continues to go well, I envision Ariella being discharged tomorrow morning."

"Tomorrow morning?" That surprised me.

"Ariella will have to be eating well and going to the bathroom before she can be discharged, but that's all. She'll be weaned off her nasal cannula [the air hose], and she still has some work to do." She smiled. "But based on what I see, she'll be discharged tomorrow."

Neither Nora nor I could fully apprehend that. There had to be more, but there was nothing more. "God had delivered our baby girl from death."

I thanked and praised God profusely and sensed His compassion for Ariella, Nora, me, and everyone involved. It was in God's grace and love for Ariella that He healed her, and He was worthy of all the glory. It was simply the hand of God; He had used ordinary people of faith to hold onto His promises and remain anchored in the fighting position of believing. I recalled some of those incredible moments on the movie screen of my mind.

Nora had exclaimed, "No, I cannot accept that. That is not God's plan for Ariella's life!"

Pastor Marshall had shared calmly and confidently, "By His stripes she is healed."

Pastor Dom had declared, "Ariella will be manifesting what Christ did two thousand years ago on the cross. She shall be healed and proclaim the Word of the Lord."

Matt had boldly proclaimed, "She shall rise on the third day."

Helen had prophesied, "Ariella means Lioness of the Lord. Ariella will live. There will be no residual or lasting effects, and she will be healed and proclaim the Word of the Lord."

Victor and Darla had said, "She shall live." And in faith, they had bought an outfit for her to wear home.

It was faith, the Word of God, and belief lived out in the lives of so many and spoken into existence by them, the community of faith. Ariella's miracle was what we had hoped and believed for when every word spoken to us on that first day went straight against it. The medical facts are what they are—facts. What we and everyone else were asking of God was a miracle that would fly in the face of evidence and do something that so many considered unlikely. And He had done it. God still does miracles, and He still answers prayer.

Ariella spent much of the day reading children's books with Mommy, recovering, and resting. She had been through so much. We settled in for the night, and Ariella was resting comfortably for the first time in these many days.

Chapter

8

Ariella Discharged and Afterward

For I delivered unto you first of all that which I also received, how that Christ died for our sins according to the scriptures; And that he was buried, and that he rose again the third day according to the scriptures.
1 Corinthians 15:3–4 (KJV)

On August 24 at 10:13 a.m., Ariella was discharged from Strong Memorial Hospital PICU in Rochester, New York. I ensured her car seat was ready and hurried back up to her room. Nora had dressed Ariella in the cute outfit Victor and Darla Garcia had given her; their words and actions had been prophetically bold.

We planned to let Ariella walk around the PICU so she and her mother and I could say our goodbyes and thanks. My mom and sister were at the house, and Yokia, Nora's sister, had gone home as well; she had been there throughout. Ariella walked down the hallway to the nurses' desk, and everyone there was so excited to see her. I think Ariella knew she was on her way out of there. She was giving them smiles; I think she was happy to see them and happy to be leaving.

As we were exiting the PICU, I reflected on Matt's words a few days before: "Ariella will rise on the third day." When I considered each twenty-four-hour period, I realized that it was on the third day that Ariella had come back to Nora and me. My God has an infinite amount of love for us, and He always has a way of bringing us back to the greatest love story of all time. It is not unlike God to bring His Word forth again and again. In this case, He did so by reminding all of us about the resurrection of His Son, Jesus. He does these things for us all.

After we said our goodbyes, gave all the hugs, and said, "Thank you" endless times to the staff of Strong Memorial Hospital's PICU, we made our way out the double doors and ran into someone special, Jen Ireland, the first nurse we encountered when we entered the PICU; she was the last person we would see there. As I mentioned earlier, we attended the same church; we learned she spoke with our pastor when Ariella had arrived. It was amazing she would be the first and last face we would see.

Jen had been supportive, praying, and present. When a news station interviewed her later, she said, "I could not believe it was the same girl from just three or four days ago. Here she was walking out of the hospital. It was God. It was a miracle! There's just no other way to explain it."

We embraced and thanked her for all she had done, for her intercessory prayer, and for walking this out with Ariella and us.

We loaded Ariella in the car and strapped her in double-checking everything. Not only at that moment but also until the present day, I am hypervigilant about her safety. I am that way with all our children, and from what my children tell me, that can be very annoying. I am especially annoying when it comes to Ariella.

Nora drove as I sat in the back with Ariella. She wanted her bottle, and I took a picture of her on my phone with me all smiles and her drinking her milk. I am not an easy person to drive with on an ordinary day, but I was probably even less easy to drive with that day. I was reminding Nora, "Thirty miles per hour, honey." "Let's go this way because of the traffic." "Slow down." "Speed up." Nora was patient and understanding; she lovingly ignored me during our drive home.

We arrived home and found notes, gifts, and lots of food. When neighbors and friends learned on the local news that Ariella was coming home, they wanted to do something, anything to support Ariella and our family. As Ariella walked into the living room, her family was there to greet her. To say there was a fuss over her would be an understatement. Ariella was home; she was safe and completely whole as if nothing had ever happened. We had dinner in her honor, and she sat in her high chair as she always does, and our family relished talking about Ariella's miracle. We were amazed with what God had done. Everyone in our family looks at Ariella through a different lens today.

In the days that followed, life got back into a routine. Ariella and Daddy watched "Baby Einstein" and "Old MacDonald" videos until exhaustion set in. We also made one-minute clips of "Ariella's Time" documenting her miraculous recovery.

Ariella still loves to see herself on video. As a family, we were able to breathe.

A few days later, we had a follow-up appointment with Dr. Marsha Gilford, Ariella's pediatrician. When Ariella walked into the office, Dr. Gilford and all the staff stopped and visited with her. Dr. Gilford had cared for all my children and was the only doctor Ariella had ever known. Physicians and nurses gathered wanting to see the young lady who had survived ten minutes underwater and experienced a miracle from God. It was such a blessing. Ariella was puzzled by all the attention, but she joyfully endured every precious moment.

Dr. Gilford shared with us, "We all saw it on the news, and I knew it was our Ariella. Just know that the PICU contacted me, and we're ready. We're so grateful for the transfer of care. We are all so happy for you!"

Dr. Gilford performed a complete physical on Ariella that confirmed what many physicians and specialists at Strong Memorial had said: "Ariella's fine. She looks great, and she's right where she needs to be. It's like nothing happened. I'll see her in a few months as usual." We were so grateful for that report.

A month or so passed, and we were getting numerous calls and requests for interviews from local networks. At the outset, I was not comfortable with that, so we tabled it for a while. Nora and I would talk from time to time about what sharing Ariella's miracle would look like. We considered the impact it could have on Ariella and our family, and we were concerned about how the story would be told. We agreed that if we told Ariella's story, we wanted to ensure that God would receive the glory for her healing. In no way were we diminishing CPR, the first responders, or the physicians' efforts, but Nora and I understood that what took place through Ariella, through all the people involved—church members, family, friends, community—was God performing a supernatural healing that caused our baby to live.

I promised God praying, "Lord, help me. I will do all I can to tell Ariella's story. Nora and I want to tell it to others. We want them to hear our testimony and give you glory for what you have done!" In time, I sensed a release and permission to move forward.

So, with that as the focus, I returned the call and email of Channel 10 (WHEC-NBC), and worked with Brent Branch, an understanding reporter. He understood what we wanted to express to the public about Ariella's miracle. We agreed to do an interview at our church in September 2016. To no one's surprise, Pastor Dom and nurse Jen Ireland participated in the interview. I would have liked to have had all the people who had spoken incredible words over Ariella to be in that interview, but these interviews would be only a few minutes long and would be edited to even fewer. We appreciated the way Brent did the story; Nora and I were grateful as the interview gave God glory for His miraculous works and served as a witness to His love for us and all humanity.

During that time, God had been dealing with me about writing this book. Nora can attest that I was constantly talking about it but also about not having the time. It was a constant tugging, almost a burden, that I had to get it down on paper. I did not have any plans past that. I had numerous notes, a couple of outlines, medical documents, and witness statements to examine and organize. I started slowly making headway on the research for a book, and soon after, we received another phone call.

In January 2017, the Christian Broadcasting Network (CBN) came across Ariella's miracle mentioned in a local news station broadcast and called us to ask about our interest in telling the world what God had done through Ariella. Again, we had the same concerns regarding the potential impact on our family. After many months of contemplation and after several conversations with the CBN staff, with each other, and our family, and after receiving wise counsel from dear friends, we agreed to share Ariella's miracle with the world.

In April 2018, Ariella's story was filmed and then televised on *The 700 Club* (CBN) on June 11, 2018. The response and outpouring have been overwhelming, and her story is encouraging the body of Christ worldwide to pray and believe. It is also touching the hearts of unbelievers who are moved by Ariella's recovery. It has opened doors to tell Ariella's story to churches and to be a support for families who experience this kind of tragedy including those who have lost children. An intense and delicate facet of Ariella's story is the comfort it brings those who have lost loved ones.

Ariella turned three on April 14, 2018, and the next month, she graduated from her two-year-old program at the YMCA in Canandaigua, New York. She knows her numbers, colors, and the entire alphabet. She is also partial to singing ABC sing-alongs, Elmo, Peppa Pig, and watching Story Online. She loves to read; she hands me one book after another.

Dr. Gilford recently saw Ariella and determined she was on target with her vocabulary and speaking at the appropriate level. Ariella and I still make videos, and she still loves to see herself on the camera. She is very athletic and has no fear. She is currently attending a preschool program for three-year-olds that started in September 2018.

Our family has a new addition. Nora and I had a baby boy in December 2017—Korban Patrick Lenney. Nora has her hands filled with caring for our children, and they have her back helping her with caring for the goats, sheep, ducks, chickens, and bees. Yes, bees. The honey is amazing. We haven't bought eggs in three years. We still attend Bethel Christian Fellowship in Rochester, New York. I still serve as a responder on the Veterans' Suicide Hotline and am deeply committed to the work I do supporting veterans.

When I started this book, I began with giving God glory for miraculously healing my baby Ariella and for His urging me to get it down on paper. I find no greater way to wrap it up except to say, "Thank you, Father, for what you did for Ariella, Nora, me, and our entire family through Ariella. We will never be the same. Thank you for healing her and for touching so many people's lives with her life. Strengthen them to remain in their fighting position of believing. I give you glory, God, for you are faithful, loving, merciful, and all powerful. All things are possible through you! You did this! You gave us Ariella's miracle! Amen."

Chapter

9

A Few Words about Miracles

My three goals for this book were to glorify God, inspire those in need of a miracle, and help others anchor themselves in the fighting position of believing. Ariella's story demands us to press further in our faith, hope, and expectation that God can and will do miracles for us all. I confess that there were moments early on during Ariella's experience when I vacillated between faith and despair. Being genuine in how we feel is not a sign of weakness; it is quite often where we need support from our Lord and others. We cannot afford to pretend to have it all together because the cost may be too great. We must ask the Lord for help to believe.

Many of us simply do not always have that overflowing measure of faith that can speak to mountains—obstacles, tragedies, diseases, or sicknesses—and make them move. I realize that many in the church consider this to be doubt, but I do not always think so. I suggest it speaks to our journey with God and what He does in us. It speaks to our human condition at times being overwhelmed by experiences that place us in neutral at best and in paralyzing shock at the worst. I was in neutral for nearly the entire first day in the hospital with Ariella. To some extent, I was in shock and dealing with guilt and regret for Ariella being hurt in the first place. When I rested my heart in Jesus, with my wife and family, I eventually moved from neutral to drive in believing God for a miracle.

Many of us have that mustard seed–sized faith and belief for what I describe as everyday needs—a new job, where to live, our hopes for our children. But there is another measure of faith altogether that only God can provide in overwhelming circumstances. The apostle Paul instructed us not to be ignorant of spiritual gifts. He described the gifts speaking directly to the gift of faith: "For to one is given by the Spirit the word of wisdom; to another the word of knowledge by the same Spirit; To another faith by the same Spirit; to another the gifts of healing by the same Spirit; To another the working of miracles" (1 Corinthians 12:8–10a KJV). Paul expressed that a supernatural gift of faith is given to some believers and perhaps in greater measure than others in certain moments. Nora had that gift of faith from the beginning regarding Ariella.

The Holy Spirit provides these gifts to the body of Christ and to those we encounter in our daily living. And please understand that this should in no way be considered a competition. Spiritual gifts are not to be competitive. Nora's incredible level of faith affected me over time, and through the grace of God, His Word, and His promises, my faith increased. I believed. The church and believers around the world would affect my faith as well.

Nora would be the first to say she does not always carry with her that incredible amount of faith in every circumstance.

God gave her that measure of faith as a gift in this very specific experience. The reality of possessing varying degrees of faith should not bring with it condemnation or guilt. It should open our thoughts to the value of making the most of our faith. It informs us to act, seek God for increased faith, and allow the supernatural and abundant measures of faith from others to gather around us and strengthen us in times of need. Faith is contagious; it forms the bridge to miracles happening.

The collective voices of supernatural faith flooded and washed over Nora and me like ocean waves. The riptide was telling us our daughter would be severely brain damaged and no longer able to walk or talk if she indeed survived. The waves of faith were instrumental in overpowering doubt and fear; they increased our faith. James 5 and Mark 16 tell us that when those among us are sick, we should call the elders in the church to lay hands on them and pray for their recovery. This obedient act occurred in Ariella's room often, and each time, in every passing hour, an increased belief and assurance manifested.

This is the community of faith's role; with a boldness and a fierce persistence, we as a church must bombard the heavens and pull on the virtue of Christ. There is a natural tendency to be paralyzed in fear, to be concerned that if we pray for a miracle or healing and it does not happen, we will ask ourselves, *What will people think?* I am challenging that notion because it is a wedge Satan creates to cause the church to be paralyzed, fearful, and of no effect.

We must be less concerned with what others think; we must do what the Lord has commanded us to do. We must surround ourselves with believers who are not worried about being embarrassed. We all must do our part unashamedly— we are to pray without ceasing, to seek the face of God in our desperation and despair and cry out to Him with the specific desires of our hearts. We must accept that this is our role and responsibility and that the rest is up to God. I want to say that again: we are to pray and prophetically speak life and God's Word to our circumstance; God alone heals and performs miracles. He certainly uses people in exercising the spiritual gifts, but the gifts come from God. The miraculous pursuit is our part; the result rests alone in the love, grace, and mercy of our God. Why this is so important to understand? Let me explain.

Shortly after Ariella's miracle, my best friend, Matt, experienced the illness and ultimately the loss of his father, Stan. Matt and I prayed for Stan's healing. His body was racked with illness, and his condition worsened daily and quickly. We prayed asking God to heal Stan. The entire family and churches to which Matt was connected prayed as well, but Stan went on to be with the Lord. There is a lot said of miracles today—why they happen for some and not others. To provide an explanation for this mystery, the early church pointed to humanity and stated that some people were not healed due to sin in their lives or in their families' lives. Undoubtedly, that left humanity confused and hurt; it did not explain why God performed miracles for some but not for others. It shifted the focus from God to humankind as responsible for its own healing. Let me point out why I feel so strongly about this with a biblical example.

In John 9, Jesus's disciples asked Him about the blind man: "Who sinned, was it him or his parents to cause this blindness?" Jesus responded, "Neither." He said that the man's blindness and subsequent healing by Jesus was to be placed on display for the world to see the works of our God. Humanity seems to have a need to place blame or to explain away things that require no explanation. We are to pray and believe, and God heals or brings home. I do not make that statement lightly. If God had brought Ariella home, that would have devastated Nora and me; our grief would have been unimaginable. Having experienced only a portion of that possible loss, I can make no comparison between that and losing a child. At varying times during Ariella's experience, I took comfort knowing that if Jesus brought her home, she would be with Him and enjoying heaven. Ariella's healing was not performed by God because she was sinless. Shifting the focus of miracles from God to humanity is flawed. Our role is to selfishly and relentlessly pray, but it is God who heals or brings home. Our lack of control and the assignment of blame serve only to take our focus off Jesus.

Concerning Stan's death, Matt did not lack faith, his family did not lack faith, and the numerous churches praying for Stan did not lack faith. No particular sin committed by Stan or his parents caused his death. The Lord in His wisdom and plan for Stan brought him home. We did our part, and God did His part for Stan. God placed Stan before us all, so we would see the glorious works of God. Many family members and friends were moved by God in Stan's room; many witnessed numerous miracles taking place all around them and in each other. Do not underestimate all that God is doing in these moments.

I recently saw *Collateral Beauty*, a movie starring Will Smith in which he and his wife experience the loss of their young daughter to cancer. While the mother was in the waiting area, a woman who represented the spirit of death told her to be sure to notice the collateral beauty that took place throughout the loss. I realize this seems so small, but as I watched that part of the movie and thought about that concept, I began to think about how God acts in our suffering. While Ariella was fighting for her life, I witnessed that collateral beauty. I witnessed Nora's incredible strength and faith. I experienced how this tragic moment brought us together as husband and wife and forever cemented us in faith. I saw the resiliency and courage of my children, who experienced the extremes of heartache and joy. I saw my parents recognize God as loving and merciful and at work in healing Ariella. I saw the faith of my sister and brother through tears and in a depth of emotions transported to a closeness with God. Death was all around us in the intensive care unit; I saw the love and unity of shared hopes and prayers of families experiencing unspeakable hardships. Nora and I saw our church, numerous pastors, and congregations operating in faith and experiencing the report of her healing. I saw physician after physician and nurse after nurse witness Ariella's miracle while being left only to credit what they could not completely understand. Finally, God placed Ariella on display for the world to see, and she was observed by more people than I could have ever comprehended.

Where else was this display observed? How might Ariella's miracle have a ripple effect on those who hear? Ariella's story was aired locally on television in Rochester, New York, and then internationally on CBN in June 2018. At first, hundreds but soon millions across the globe were touched by her story. I have given a great deal of thought about the collateral beauty through Ariella's experience and am amazed at what I learn through every testimony. Many days removed, I am so grateful for seeing God placing His miraculous works in Ariella on display.

Like many of you, I am astonished by miracles. I do not understand the when and who, but I know what I experienced through Ariella. Nevertheless, one lesson learned from Ariella's miracle is the importance of guarding our minds against negative voices that attempt to penetrate our faith. Spending too much time on the whens and whos removes us from exercising our role of praying and seeking God for the miraculous. Dwelling on the negative reports from even trusted authorities can paralyze us. I struggled with the whens and whos, and I could not easily dismiss the input of the physicians who told me to prepare for Ariella's death. God's grace through His voice and words coupled with numerous voices of the community of faith overpowered those negative voices. I took the fighting position of believing. Again, we must watch out for the voices that attempt to penetrate our faith. Let me provide you with a biblical example that has ministered to my heart since Ariella's miracle.

In Mark 5, when Jesus arrived in the Galilee area, a ruler from a synagogue fell to his knees and pleaded with Jesus to come to his home to lay hands on his twelve-year-old daughter and heal her. He expressed to Jesus the dire nature of her illness. Jesus agreed to go with him and started walking surrounded by a crowd of people.

Now, while they were making their way to Jairus's home, a woman who had been hemorrhaging for years heard Jesus was coming and made it her life's largest moment to just touch Him and be healed. She pressed through the crowd and touched Jesus's clothes, and He realized someone with faith had sought His power and healing virtue. When Jesus wheeled around and asked, "Who touched me?" the disciples were bewildered because of the crowd. How could they know who specifically had drawn upon His virtue? A woman came forward and told Jesus everything! She let it pour out, and after Jesus heard her story, He told her, "Your faith has made you whole."

As Jesus was finishing His conversation with the woman, one of Jairus's men from the synagogue came and told Jairus, "Your daughter is dead. Why trouble the master any further?" Jesus overheard what the man had said but ignored him. He told Jairus, "Don't be afraid. Just believe."

A couple points to consider: Jesus ignored the voice that penetrated Jairus's faith. Jesus's response warns us to guard our minds and ignore these voices. In our case, it was "death, severe brain damage, never be the same"; in Jairus's case, it was plainly death.

When we desperately seek Jesus, He is moved by our faith in Him and compassion. Hebrews 11:6 (NIV) tells us, "And without faith it is impossible to please God." God is pleased by faith. Hebrews 11 clarifies that for people to even come to God, they must believe in Him and that He exists. The Bible is filled with examples of men and women who have faith but imperfectly. The latter part of Hebrews 11:6 informs us that because of that belief, He rewards those who earnestly seek Him. What we witness in scripture is a resilient and persistent faith. It is important to understand the heart of God in this matter. He certainly responds to faith, but it seems He also recognizes that humanity's faith is imperfect. Jesus expressed this sentiment to His disciples numerous times asking them why they had such little faith. Faith is necessary for salvation. God thankfully appears to those who believe in Him; He responds to our cries when we fear or struggle. Jairus is the perfect example of someone who believed in Him and desperately sought Jesus for the miraculous even when he was struggling.

In Jairus's example, Jesus healed the daughter based on the "possible" faith of the father (Mark 5). Jesus told Jairus to not be afraid and believe. To believe. We can conclude that when Jairus learned of his daughter's death, he was afraid and lacked faith based on Jesus's instruction to Jairus not to be afraid and believe. Jairus was likely terrified when he learned his daughter was dead, and he may have thought that the possibility of the miraculous was over. I raise this to your awareness because if you are seeking God for a miracle, you are demonstrating faith in Him that He can answer your prayers. Consider a few miracles Jesus performed.

Jesus healed the paralytic not because of his faith but because of the faith of the four who carried him in through the roof (Mark 2). Faith was instrumental but not necessarily from the one who was healed. Jesus saw their faith and had compassion.

Jesus raised Lazarus from the dead. As you can imagine, it was not Lazarus's faith (he was dead) and it was not necessarily the faith of his family, who were angry with Jesus for taking so long (John 11). Mary, Lazarus's sister, did not appear to lose faith in Jesus but rather in her brother living. When Jesus saw Mary's grief, He was moved by compassion; He wept and raised Lazarus from the dead.

Jesus healed the ear of the soldier Peter wounded, but it did not appear faith was involved at all (John 18). The soldier was most likely not a believer in Christ, and it is a pretty safe bet that Peter did not pray for him to be healed.

Jesus fed 5,000 people (Matthew 15), and that did not appear to require any faith from anyone. The disciples were overwhelmed not knowing what to do. Jesus was moved by compassion and performed a miracle with a few loaves of bread and fish.

If miracles and healing depend on our level of faith alone, we are in deep trouble. If God depended on humankind's faith to heal and save, humankind would only need to turn to itself. Humanity is incapable of conjuring up enough faith to heal itself. God requires us to seek and rely on Him, to believe in Him and not in our abilities.

We have no goodness, no sin, no issue that determines the answer to our prayers for miracles and healing. Of course, we strive to be good Christians and endeavor to avoid sin and live good lives, but these efforts alone do not dictate God's answering our prayers for miracles. The scriptures are filled with God answering the prayers of sinful people. The miraculous rests solely on His sovereign love and mercy. I realize that was a departure from our text, but I feel it was an important one. You and I cannot dictate miracles, but we can bombard God with our petitions; what He will do for one, He can and will do for another.

Picking back up on our text with Jairus—when Jesus arrived at Jairus's home, professional mourners were weeping and crying as they perceived the girl was dead. Jesus recognized their disingenuous and purely ceremonial spirit and rebuked them for that; He instructed them to leave. When we are going through the most horrific experiences of our lives, we do not want to fill our space with any purely ceremonial spirit; we want and need prayer warriors who are unapologetic and believe in God with fervor and determination and believe He can answer prayer. Jesus went as far as to kick the ceremonial people out of the area. He would allow only a few of His closest disciples and the parents into the home, people who believed for the miracle and for whom He had compassion.

Take note that nowhere in the text did Jairus instantaneously become unafraid and gain unimaginable belief. It appears that Jairus believed when he sought Jesus out, but after the men told him his daughter had died, Jairus's faith took a hit. What we do know is that from the very beginning, Jairus believed Jesus could do it! This was where I was with Ariella; I knew God could heal her, but I just didn't have that immediate and complete assurance. And for several hours of the first day with Ariella, I walked as Jairus walked—as a bystander to what Jesus was going to do. What I could do was desperately seek Jesus.

Why do you trouble the Master? Jesus is the way, the truth, the life; He is the only one who can save you and your children, who can heal, deliver, and perform the miraculous. Only Jesus can save loved ones from disease, tragedy, addiction, and affliction. Jesus is drawn by our faith and subsequent belief for the miraculous; He is drawn to our brokenness and suffering. Being this type of seeker of God is at times uncomfortable, costly, painful, and exhausting. But in it is the very power of God on earth.

Jesus walked into where the girl was lying and told her, "Little girl, get up!" And the girl arose and walked around the room. Can you imagine what Jairus thought? Can you imagine what joy he experienced? I can see him crying uncontrollably, holding his wife, and hugging his daughter. I see him drawing close to Jesus praising and thanking Him. I see the disciples astonished yet again at the power of Christ in raising the dead to life. I can also see the ceremonial spirit outside the doors of the home when it was shared that the Savior had raised the girl from the dead.

There will always be scoffers, those who deny the power of Christ, and of course Satan, the enemy of our souls. He is the source of many of the negative voices that attempt to penetrate our faith. This impacts not only the miraculous but also our everyday lives and most assuredly our sense of self-esteem and self-worth. Satan stands ready to accuse every church, every pastor and leader, every believer, every parent, every child, and every warrior, and he does so daily. To have been a fly on that young girl's wall or to have walked with Jesus as He exited that home would have been priceless; Satan and his minions would have shrunk in His presence absolutely defeated.

When I had the spiritual dream on the morning of Ariella's accident and the second dream in the hospital, it was impressed upon me that Satan had directly attacked Ariella. In the time since, this warning has been brought to me several times. Satan remains the adversary and seeks how he can take her life. I do not live in constant fear of this knowledge; I vigilantly protect Ariella and the purpose I believe God has planned for her. And God's plans and power overcome the world.

In Jairus's experience (Mark 5), we witness God's unlimited power. The story of the woman who was hemorrhaging was dropped in the middle of Jairus's efforts. I believe God was showing us critical elements to His omnipresence, omniscience, and omnipotence. Jairus's daughter was dead, and on their way, Jesus was interrupted by the woman. Jesus healed many people with complete understanding of their needs, and His power is undeniable. He is not limited by time, circumstances, or the severity of an illness, issue, or event. This is for you and me to receive from the Lord. He can heal all things, anytime, anywhere for anyone who seeks Him.

In Ariella's case, Jesus was not troubled by her having been underwater and without oxygen for ten minutes. With the hemorrhaging woman, He was not intimated by the fact that she had had the issue for twelve years. In Jairus's little girl, Jesus was not troubled that she had died; He can heal multiple people at multiple times and in multiple locations. That is what He does today. Our role is to plead as Jairus did for Jesus to heal. We are to cut through all the negative voices and obstacles and touch God by every means possible. We are to believe with our measures of faith that He can and will do it; the rest is up to Him. We are to do this as a collective body, the church of the living Christ operating as a warrior team not paralyzed by fear but believing that God is able.

Miracles can happen anywhere, anytime, and in any circumstance no matter how dire. Quite simply, to answer the man's question to Jairus, "Your daughter is dead, why trouble the Master?" Christ's love, compassion, and power are the reasons we trouble the Master! We fight the fight while there is time. We fight by troubling the Master from our fighting position of believing. And He is not troubled at all.

Chapter

10

Questions to Consider about Ariella's Miracle

1. Pastor Marshall responded to Patrick's and Nora's phone call with faith and calm confidence. His faith increased their faith and hope. How does the faith of others impact you when you have a need in your life?

_____

_____

_____

2. When Pastor Dom referred to Ariella's healing as being "manifested today for what Jesus did two thousand years ago at the cross," (John 3:16) what event was he talking about? How has that event affected your life?

_____

_____

_____

3. The Word of God is life; it contains incredible power. When the community of faith proclaims it, it is sent to perform mighty works. When you speak it in faith over your life, the lives of others, or circumstances, it can move mountains. Jesus said, "Truly I tell you, if you have faith as small as a mustard seed, you can say to this mountain, 'Move from here to there,' and it will move. Nothing will be impossible for you" (Matthew 17:20 NIV). Can you provide an example in the book when someone spoke the word of God over Ariella? What situation in your life can you speak the Word of God to?

_____

_____

_____

4. Prophetic prayer and words of knowledge were shared with Patrick and Nora over the course of these days. Helen prophesied that Ariella would fully recover without any residual effects. Matt stated that Ariella would rise on the third day. How do you reconcile the specificity of their words and the outcome?

_____

_____

_____

5. How does Ariella's miracle affect the way you feel about miracles?

_____

_____

_____

Chapter

11

Scriptures on Miracles and Healing

He is thy praise, and he is thy God, that hath done for thee these great and terrible things, which thine eyes have seen. (Deuteronomy 10:21 KJV)

Behold, I am the Lord, the God of all flesh: is there any thing too hard for me? (Jeremiah 32:27 KJV)

And he said, The things which are impossible with men are possible with God. (Luke 18:27 KJV)

Jesus said unto him, If thou canst believe, all things are possible to him that believeth. (Mark 9:23 KJV)

And Jesus said unto them, Because of your unbelief: for verily I say unto you, If ye have faith as a grain of mustard seed, ye shall say unto this mountain, Remove hence to yonder place; and it shall remove; and nothing shall be impossible unto you. (Matthew 17:20 KJV)

But Jesus beheld them, and said unto them, With men this is impossible; but with God all things are possible. (Matthew 19:26 KJV)

I would seek unto God, and unto God would I commit my cause: Which doeth great things and unsearchable; marvellous things without number: (Job 5:8–9 KJV)

And now, Lord, behold their threatenings: and grant unto thy servants, that with all boldness they may speak thy word, By stretching forth thine hand to heal; and that signs and wonders may be done by the name of thy holy child Jesus. And when they had prayed, the place was shaken where they were assembled together; and they were all filled with the Holy Ghost, and they spake the word of God with boldness. (Acts 4:29–31 KJV)

Now unto him that is able to do exceeding abundantly above all that we ask or think, according to the power that worketh in us, Unto him be glory in the church by Christ Jesus throughout all ages, world without end. Amen. (Ephesians 3:20–21 KJV)

Chapter

12

Acknowledgments

Nora and I thank all the first responders from Chili, New York, Fire and Rescue; all responding police and paramedics; and Strong Memorial Hospital ER and PICU staff for their tireless efforts. We also thank every prophetic voice that spoke into Ariella's life, every pastor, church, and believer who prayed, laid hands on her, and held services with her as the focus.

We believe that the avalanche of prayers, praying of the scriptures, words of knowledge, and prophetic utterances were instrumental in her healing and that God caused her recovery.

We are so grateful for the love and support of family, friends, community, and neighbors who supported us during this ordeal.

Last, we thank our Lord and Savior Jesus Christ for without His grace, mercy, love, and healing, Ariella's miracle would not have been possible.

Chapter

13

About Nora and Patrick Lenney

Patrick is a retired Marine with more than twenty-three years of active and honorable service. He served in Iraq in 2005. He has been in ministry since 1997, and he pastored his first church while stationed in Japan. He has a master's degree in social work from Roberts Wesleyan College and is a licensed master social worker in New York State. He has a master's degree in divinity from Northeastern Seminary in Rochester, New York. He and Nora attend Bethel Christian Fellowship in Rochester, New York. He still serves as a responder on the Veterans' Suicide Hotline in Canandaigua, New York.

Nora has a Bachelor of Science degree from the State University of Brockport and has specialized in case management for those in need of care. She is currently staying at home caring for their children, raising the animals on their hobby farm, and tending her garden. She has been a member of the prophetic ministry at Bethel Christian Fellowship and is an anointed prophetic voice in ministry.

Patrick and Nora are a blended family with nine children. Oldest is Vance (twenty-eight), Jacob (twenty-two), Ajanee (twenty), Solomon (eighteen), Ysaiahs (sixteen), Ethan (fifteen), Gianna (seven), Ariella (three), and Korban (one year old). They enjoy their home and land, going to church, sports, caring for their animals (goats, sheep, ducks, chickens, and bees), and spending time together.

Chapter

14

Photographs of the Lenney Family

Ariella playing with her blocks

Ariella and Patrick looking out over Canandaigua Lake, New York

Ariella and Nora playing outside

Ariella picking berries off the tree

Ariella laughing with her siblings while playing in the front yard

Ariella showing her speed running to Nora

The Lenney family pruning their newly planted tree

Nora and Patrick Lenney

Ariella and her sister Gianna hanging out at
their favorite rock in the front yard

The Lenney family walking across their yard
to look at the neighbor's horses

References

Christian Broadcasting Network televised on June 11, 2018, on *The 700 Club*, http://www1.cbn.com/parents-hold-promise-miracle; retrieved July 30, 2018.

Channel 10 (WHEC) story: "Chili baby girl makes 'miraculous' recovery after falling in pool," https://www.youtube.com/watch?v=KlaMOjP6nJM&t=2s

Scripture references (NIV and KJV) taken from https://www.biblegateway.com; retrieved on July 30, 2018.

Some names and identifying details have been changed to protect the privacy of individuals.

Photography by Tom Patros.

As a producer for *The 700 Club*, I have the opportunity to travel the country and document people's stories; be they salvations, healings, or miracles, it is amazing to see how God is moving in the world today. *Ariella's Miracle* has been one of my favorite stories to witness. Patrick's honest and thought-provoking account of what the family went through during Ariella's accident will touch your heart.

Patrick and Nora are a couple who truly love God and seek Him out at every turn. So when they faced this life-threatening trial, they knew their best option was to turn to Him. And God showed up in a mighty way. *Ariella's Miracle* demonstrates the importance and power of prayer. God is still listening. God is still answering prayer. God is still working miracles. *Ariella's Miracle* will strengthen your faith, deepen your walk with God, and show you that nothing is too hard for God to handle.

Edward Heath
Senior Producer
The 700 Club (CBN)

Ariella's Miracle is a story that will strengthen your faith and resolve to see God's kingdom come and His will to be done on earth as it is in heaven. It is a story of God's intervention via a dream, prophetic words, and the prayers of many of God's children that turned tragedy into triumph for the Lenney family. It is a true picture of the power of faith, hope, and love as well as a testimony to the power of God at work through the mediation of the saints as they hold onto the truth and power of God's Word.

Pastor Ron Domina
Bethel Christian Fellowship
Rochester, New York

For more information, go to https://ariellasmiracle.com
Email: info@ariellasmiracle.com

Printed in the United States
By Bookmasters